CU00751740

A Chairman's Tale

A Chairman's Tale

SIR NIGEL RUDD

LUME BOOKS

LUME BOOKS

This edition published in 2022 by Lume Books

ISBN 978-1-83901-463-5

Typeset using Atomik ePublisher from Easypress Technologies

www.lumebooks.co.uk

Printed and bound in Great Britain by Clays Ltd, Elcograf S.p.A

Contents

Foreword

The idea for writing this book came after a number of friends suggested that my experiences over four decades in business would make an informative read. I was sceptical at first, but over time I came around to thinking that my time at the very top of UK corporate life would be of interest not only to my family, but also to those interested in how corporate life has changed over five decades.

I have read a number of autobiographies written by prominent businessmen and women, and I knew that I did not want this book to be a lecture on how to be successful or an exercise in pushing a particular business theory. However, I have never kept a diary, so have had to rely on memory and press cuttings for much of the detail.

This is predominantly a chronicle of my life in business and does not cover many of the wonderful times I have had with friends and family, golfing, skiing, shooting or simply enjoying wonderful holidays around the world. When I have read other books of this kind, I always tended to skip such sections because they are only relevant to those who were involved. Therefore, in this introduction I want to thank all those people who have made my journey through life such a pleasure.

The main support to me has, of course, been my wife Lesley. Our partnership has lasted well over 50 years, and without her support, particularly in the early days, none of this would have happened. She does not feature prominently in the book simply because at no time has she wanted to be actively involved in business. In fact, a friend of mine called her the perfect corporate wife – a wonderful foil, always there when needed but never letting her real thoughts on people who I've dealt with, or deals that I've done, be publicly known. Privately, of course, she has expressed her views and her judgment of people was almost always spot on.

One of Lesley's great successes in life is to have brought up three wonderful children. I was often away for long periods on business trips and when our children were young, life was hard. Money was short – when I first went into business on my own, we even had to sell her car to meet some bills. Yet, throughout my career, she has always provided me with the stability and space I needed to achieve my business goals.

I have many great friends and it would be wrong to single a few of them out here and risk offending others. They know who they are, and I would like to thank them for their friendship, occasional advice and above all their loyalty to me and my family over the years.

Finally, a big thank you to Andrew Lorenz, who has patiently put together the story from my odd jottings and semi-literate command of the English Language.

Nigel Rudd
April 2022

1

Starting Out

It seemed a very long way up to the eighth floor, but I took the stairs in my stride. I was a young man on a mission: 25 years old, the youngest-ever qualified chartered accountant in England, and official trouble-shooter for a well-known public company. That day, I was earning my corn.

I was about to confront a truly hard case. The company I worked for owned 75% of a former private company which for months had told us nothing – it had supplied no financial information at all, not even the most basic cash flow information and profit and loss reports. I was at their head office in north London to put a stop to this nonsense.

The eighth was also the top floor. There to meet me was the company's chairman, a grizzled, take-no-prisoners Irishman, along with one of his right-hand men. This other guy was huge: he had fingers the size of bananas.

Undaunted, I confronted them. "You aren't producing management accounts," I told them straight. "We control this business and I've come here with authorisation to join your board. I want you to call a board meeting to elect me."

They didn't reply. Instead, the big bloke opened the window, then picked up my briefcase and threw it out. When it hit the ground – which took a little while – the papers scattered everywhere. Then he said simply: "If you don't **** off, you're next."

As they say in business schools, I recognised that my leverage was limited. Chastened, I promptly beat a hasty retreat to the car park, salvaged what remained of my briefcase, and bolted back to head office where I told my bosses that "I don't think I'm going there again!" We ended up selling the business back to the Irishman at a significant loss.

I've defenestrated a few executives in my career – figuratively speaking. Some of them had to go without much ceremony, and they didn't thank me for it. But the shock treatment I received from the men in north London was something else.

I got over it pretty quickly – filing it mentally under "colourful experiences" – because even by that early stage of my business life, I had been to many places and seen quite a lot. In that respect, I was a lucky man: your average young accountant would have been shackled to a desk, poring over numbers on a page. I had read my share of spreadsheets, and that taught me financial analysis. But I also saw real businesses in action: the good, bad and ugly. Above all, I learned an awful lot about people. And those lessons were the most valuable of all.

My life might have been very different, had my educational career had taken another turn. I was born on New Year's Eve 1946 – the day before the National Coal Board was created. My parents were quite elderly: my father was 50 years old when I was born, so there was a tremendous age gap between us.

My father was real working class, the son of a limestone miner in Dudley. In the First World War, he saw service in Gallipoli, Greece and Egypt with the Sherwood Foresters. He was a motorcycle dispatch rider, moving between trenches, so he was very lucky to survive. Like most of the men who suffered the trauma of that war, he never, ever talked about it with me. Years later, just before he died, I offered to take my parents on holiday, knowing that my mother had never been abroad. He just stared at me and said: "I don't want to go abroad. The last time I did, all they wanted to do was kill me."

He had a rough time during the Depression of the 1930s. His first wife died very young of cancer, without having had any children.

He lived in the Black Country and, like millions of others, was out of work for long periods. He eventually trained as a weights and measures inspector (we'd call it trading standards, today) and got a job with Derbyshire County Council in Derby, so he moved there. He met my mother and they were married in 1938.

With my brother Graham

My mother was 10 years younger than my father. She was half-Irish and a very forceful character. She came – or at least she *claimed* that she came – from an upper middle class Dublin family on her mother's side. The story went that the family's wealth disappeared in the 1930s in a bank crash. Her father was a clerk working for the London, Midland and Scottish railway company in Derby.

My elder brother Graham was born in February 1945 and I came along 22 months later. We lived in a three-bedroom house in the town. My childhood could be described as typical for someone born just after the war. I remember rationing, particularly of sweets. Any kind of meat was a real treat and chicken was a luxury. Salmon was unheard of, but we seemed to have good supplies of other fish, especially on a Friday. By the standards of the day, we were definitely not poor and there was never an occasion when I felt there was a shortage of food. But there was nothing extra.

Our holidays were spent at my spinster aunt's two-bedroom flat in Bournemouth. The four of us crammed in together after the marathon eight-hour drive from Derby, a trip broken only by a picnic in a field somewhere in Oxfordshire. Graham and I sat in the back of our Austin A40, betting on how long it would take for the ash at the end of my father's cigarette to fall off onto his lap.

In the garden with Dad and Graham

My mother thought Bournemouth was so far south of Derby that it was on a different continent, so we always spent the first few days acclimatising and were not allowed to go into the sea or even put our bathing trunks on. My trunks were woollen and when we were eventually allowed in, they weighed so much that they ended up around my knees!

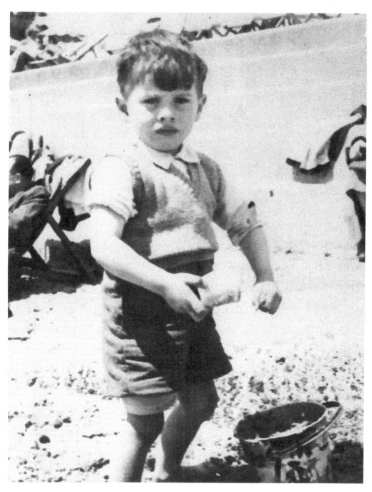

On Bournemouth beach

The infamous swimming shorts!

There was no money in the family – when he retired in 1963, my father was earning £20 a week – no history of education, and very few books in the house. But there was a huge amount of aspiration. My parents were lower middle class Conservatives with a capital 'C' and their attitude to life was: *Our two boys have got to do better than we have.* They were very ambitious for Graham and me – we felt that we had to succeed.

Graham has had a very successful career. After qualifying as an accountant, he was for many years chief executive of the company that made the hand cleanser, Swarfega. He then had a career investing in small and medium-sized businesses. He is a pillar of Derbyshire society, having been a deputy lieutenant and then high sheriff, and we were all delighted when he was recently awarded the MBE in recognition of his public service. I think that my parents, even with their high aspirations for us, could not have envisaged our success in life.

At the age of five, I went to Markeaton Infants school and at eight I went to Ashgate Primary. This school was in the notorious west end of Derby, and children from seriously poor families were my classmates. With my parents owning their own home – bought just before the war for £800 – I was at the upper end of the pupils' social scale. It was pretty rough, with frequent fights in the playground and on the way home. Corporal punishment was commonplace, but I never felt it harmed me in any way. Most of the time I probably deserved it and a cane across the fingers didn't hurt for long. The school had no grass – only tarmac – and sports were played on a nearby recreation ground.

With my stamp collection

Ashgate had one great advantage over many similar schools: our Welsh headmaster, Mr Meredith, had an amazing ability to get the best out of the boys. So much so that, despite being in a pretty deprived area, Ashgate had the highest pass rate for the 11-plus in the whole of Derby. I duly passed my 11-plus but, much to my parents' disappointment, was awarded a place at Bemrose Grammar School rather than the much smaller and more prestigious Derby

Grammar School. Bemrose had only been founded in the 1930s and was named after the then-mayor of Derby, whereas Derby GS was much older and had loads of famous old boys. The new school was a couple of miles from home, so I started off by walking there and made a big fuss about having a bike. A new one was out of the question so eventually, after a year or two, a second-hand Palm Beach Tourer was purchased. My pride and joy.

Ashgate Primary School cricket team. Note: no grass

In the first year at Bemrose, pupils were not put into sets according to ability. There were 120 boys in four classes and at the end of the year we took exams to determine which set we would be in for the second year. I am probably slightly dyslexic, which hampered me, but to make matters worse, for some reason the streaming decision was taken purely on the basis of ability shown in foreign languages. I was, and still am, incapable of learning languages. It's just a blind spot.

With my new, second-hand bike

I was therefore placed in the bottom stream. All three streams above that took French, the top boys took Russian as well, the next set German and the third Spanish. My set was called 2MS – which stood for mechanical science. Mechanical science was woodwork and metalwork. My only memory of the woodwork class was when I was punished for larking about at the back. The master took hold of me by the tie and nailed that tie to a bench for the rest of the lesson. In this day and age, he would probably be fired but back then, such treatment of pupils was normal. I remember the humiliation of being bent over, with the rest of the class in stitches. I have never been very handy around the house and I trace that shortcoming back to this disturbing event.

However, in the end of year exams, I came top of the form and was promoted to the third stream. And after another two terms, I was moved up to the second stream. We all have teachers we remember, and there was one teacher at this point who made a huge difference to my life. He was a maths master called Mr Calvert – nicknamed 'Eddie' after the famous trumpeter of that time.

First day at grammar school

Eddie Calvert stood out from the other masters for one good reason: he had not been to university and had come into teaching late, so he was the only master who did not wear a black gown (which signified that the owner had a degree). He was an excellent teacher and, after one maths lesson, he asked me to stay behind for a chat. He had been looking at my work and told me in no uncertain terms that I was cruising and that, if I applied myself more, I could be a serious mathematician. During the next few weeks, he gave me extra work over and above class work, and spent time after school helping me.

At the end of that year the headmaster, Dr W. R. C. Chapman, called me into his study. Eddie Calvert was there. The head said they were going to recommend that for the next year, I would be placed in the top form of the fourth year. This was the prestigious lower trans: its members were all scholarship boys and they took their 'O' levels at the end of that year, a year ahead of the rest. They also told me that this would make me the only boy in the school to have climbed through all four streams. Eddie's parting words to me were: "Don't let me down."

The next year was tough because I was now in the company of seriously bright boys. I was in the middle of the class for most subjects, bottom by a long way in French but very good in sciences and second or third in maths. I inherited that ability from my father – he was highly numerate and could add up three columns of figures at once. In the end, I got good 'O' levels – I even scraped a pass in French. As a result, I skipped the fifth year and went straight into the first year of sixth form where I studied maths, along with economics and geography.

I was 15 years of age and growing in confidence. I loved all kinds of sport, although I was very average in most of them. Bemrose was a soccer school and despite being on the short side, I was the house goalkeeper. When the school started to play a bit of rugby, the master in charge wanted me in the team. I have always been very thick set and he thought me ideal for the front row. My mother wouldn't hear of it – she thought rugby was dangerous – so I refused the offer. I regret it in some ways, but in my old age I have none of the back, shoulder and knee problems that I see in my friends who played rugby in their youth. So maybe she had a point.

The one game I excelled at was tennis, and I owed that to my mother. She thought it would help me to be socially mobile, and when I was about 10 years old, she spotted a newspaper advert from the local branch of the Lawn Tennis Association, promoting a series of coaching sessions in the nearby park. My mother had played tennis when she was a girl, and she hoped I would be interested. I duly turned up for coaching with a racket borrowed from a neighbour, and really enjoyed it. The lessons were free and I signed up for a course in the summer holidays.

The Derbyshire under-15 team before playing Nottinghamshire

I took to the game immediately, joined a club and started to take it quite seriously. Bemrose had a team and, perhaps because it was such a minority sport, I was one of the top six players from the age of 12. We had a very good group of really talented players: the stars were the Jarrett brothers Roger and Clive, who played at junior Wimbledon. They had a much younger sibling, Andrew, who went on to play in the Davis Cup and later became a Wimbledon referee, running the famous tournament.

The Bemrose Grammar School tennis team

I played for Derbyshire at Under 15 level and was runner up in the county championship at that age. When I left school and started work, I didn't have the time to take things further but I played for the local team in Derby and my doubles partner on many occasions was a young engineer at Rolls-Royce, the largest and most famous company in the town (Derby only became a city in the 1960s). His name was Ralph Robins, and he ultimately became Sir Ralph, chief executive and then chairman of Rolls. I soon learned to appreciate his management skills: he said to me before one match: "You do the running at the back of the court and I'll take care of the net!" Very good advice – get others to do the grunt work and concentrate on the strategy. Today, Ralph and I sit together when we go to watch Derby County. He's a great man.

With my 'O' levels out of the way, I had to decide on my next step. The conventional route to self-improvement would have been to stay in the system and then go to university. But my mother believed that the key was to enter a profession and start making money at the earliest opportunity. She worked as a clerk in an accounting office, and she told me and my brother that "I've never met a badly-off accountant." Her determination and my father's financial circumstances caused major conflict with my headmaster.

Ever since my good 'O' levels, the headmaster had assumed that I would take my 'A' levels and apply for university. But in the November of my first term in the sixth form, my father called me aside and said: "You are going to do the same as your brother" – who had left school at 16 and gone to work for a firm of accountants. I can't remember arguing with him. My father was 65 and about to retire on a pension of £600 a year with no other savings.

Dad's retirement

The school, when informed, was furious. Dr Chapman came to see my parents at our house, which was almost unheard of. I remember that night vividly: he was ushered into the front room and I was asked to stay in the kitchen. I could hear the shouting. He told my mother and father that it was wrong to take me away from school, that I could go to Oxbridge. "You are going to ruin his life," he said. My father replied that he could not afford to send me to university. Of course, there was no history in the family of knowing anything about grants and although the school must have known, for some reason it was never discussed.

Many years later, when I was having a fair degree of success at Williams, I took a call from the president of Derby Rotary Club. They wanted me to join them for a dinner in honour of one of the oldest members – to do a bit of a 'This Is Your Life' for him. The member was Dr Chapman – my old headmaster. We had a great evening and he recalled the dramatic visit to our home. He accepted that missing out on university had not ruined my life, but he still insisted that he had been right to try and persuade my father to change his mind.

I left school at the end of November, a month before my sixteenth birthday, and was frogmarched to sign up as an accountant. I know I was the youngest-ever chartered accountant in England because I signed my Articles at 15 years and 11 months, which was on the edges of being illegal: you weren't supposed to start Articles until you were aged 16. I know that's true because I still have the document – and it clearly states that the minimum age to sign Articles was 16. I duly qualified five years later when I was still only 20 – but they didn't let me into the Institute of Chartered Accountants until I reached 21.

First date with Lesley (I hired the dinner jacket)

From the outset, I was lucky. My father had a contact at R. J. Weston & Co., a medium-sized practice in Derby, so I joined them. It was hard work and paid very little, but I really enjoyed my accountancy training.

Articled clerks in those days were mainly from monied families. Only a few years before my time, the pupil actually paid the firm a premium for the privilege of being trained. I was paid £1.50 a week to start with and when I finished five years later, I was getting £5.50 a week. I was working five-and-a-half days a week and taking a correspondence course at night, so it was hard and left me time for very little social life.

However, I became treasurer of the Derby chartered accountants' society. We once organised a barbecue and it was there that I met Lesley. She came from a very well-known Derby family of high-class grocers – a class of business that was eventually wiped out by the supermarkets. We were both aged 18 and she had just returned from a year of schooling in Switzerland. I was on the door that night and Lesley was with a friend. I rather liked the look of her, so I let them in free. We got on very well and agreed to meet again the following week.

That was in 1964, so we have now been together for well over 50 years and have three great children and seven grandchildren. It's a bit of a joke in Derby that I married into a class higher than my own. It's true, of course – when we married in 1969, I had about £100 to my name and the deposit for the house we bought came from her grandmother, who died just before we married. She gave us a great financial start to married life.

Our wedding

When I qualified, Weston & Co. offered me a job as an audit manager. I didn't like auditing, but the great thing about working and qualifying in the practice was that you saw everything; our clients included small public companies, but were mostly medium-sized and larger private companies in a range of traditional Midlands industries – construction, foundries, engineering. So, in my late teens I was going around looking at all these businesses from an auditor's standpoint, seeing who was making money and who wasn't, forming what I suppose was a very immature view of management and how things got done, but also working out in my own brain what was successful and what wasn't.

My mother wanted me to become a partner in the firm after I qualified, which I could have done and which would have suited her aspirations for me in terms of social standing. She was, as I have said, a real driving force and had great ambitions for her two boys. Sometimes, it felt as if it was the three of us against the world. On this occasion, though, I resisted her idea: I didn't want to be a practising accountant, I wanted to work in business. So I joined a construction and plant hire company called Egan Contractors, which needed a financial controller; they only had a bookkeeper until then. Armed with my newly-acquired chartered accountant status, I got this job at the age of 21.

The company was run by a couple of Irishmen, one of whom couldn't read or write but both of whom were very crafty, really smart. I had been there for about a year when they decided to sell the business. I negotiated the sale to the London & Northern Group (L&N), a public company run by a well-known Scottish entrepreneur, Jock Mackenzie.

Within months of the sale, the Irishmen took their money and retired. That caused a huge upheaval, because they had created the company; as far as the staff were concerned, it was their business. So, L&N asked me to step in and run it, which I did. I was 22 and hadn't a clue about how to go about it, but I operated on instinct and on what I had learned from my auditing experience.

I managed to stabilise the business and we started to do quite well, which earned me my spurs with L&N. They were one of the first conglomerates – holding companies which bought smaller companies in many different industries. They never did much due diligence – they just got bigger and wider-spread. Many of the companies they bought were absolute rubbish, and they asked me to sort these out. I spent the next four or five years doing that, travelling all over the UK and Ireland: my nickname in the company was 'the fireman', because I was sent in to douse crises. I spent a year in Dublin turning one business around, travelling out every Monday and coming home the following Saturday. Some of the businesses I saw were really strange – they were what you might call 'tasty', like the one I have already described in north London!

Eventually, I reached a point where I'd seen enough dodgy businesses and wanted to do something different. The last straw was an open cast coal company in north-east England, which seemed to be doing very well, despite paying a royalty per tonne to the National Coal

The young businessman

Board (NCB). When I delved a little, I discovered why. Most of the coal was removed at night, when the NCB checkers were at home asleep. The coal was delivered by road to the Central Electricity Generating Board's power stations in the Midlands, and I was quietly told by one of our guys to take a close look at a wagon which was all loaded up. Before the operators reached the weighbridge, they would pump hundreds of gallons of water into the wagon to inflate the weight and falsify the tonnage reading so that the NCB would not question the amount of coal delivered. After this, I decided to find a different line of work.

My opportunity arose when L&N bought a Midlands housebuilder called Bardolin, which in turn owned a struggling house building and contracting company in South Wales, C. Price & Sons. L&N fired the executives and asked me to go in and take over. I went with a guy who was an operations expert.

I knew it was going to be a long job, so I moved the family there with me. By that time – 1976 – we had two sons, Tim and Edward, and our daughter Jennifer would be born whilst we were in South Wales. We lived in Abergavenny, where we met my lawyer's daughter, Penelope Clark, who turned out to be a rather interesting individual. She used to go off on exchange visits to France, and on one of them she met François Fillon – whom she later married and became the Gaullist candidate for French President in the 2017 election.

By now the British economy was becoming seriously troubled, and L&N decided that they needed to raise cash. They therefore planned either to close or to sell C. Price. I thought, *this isn't a bad business*. It effectively had no value, because the cost of closing it or the price at which it could be sold would wipe out whatever residual value it did have. So in Autumn 1978, the year before Margaret Thatcher was elected, I went to L&N with Roger Edwards, a builder I knew, and asked them: "Would you sell me the company?" They said: "If you can do it before December 31, then OK" – they wanted to wrap up the deal before the end of their financial year because the prevailing accounting standards said that if you sold a company during your trading year, you could deconsolidate it in the year-end figures. Because Price was losing money, L&N could thereby get the losses off their P&L.

We met their deadline, completing the purchase in November. They gave me £10,000 compensation for my being 'fired' and I paid it back to them for the business.

Incidentally, the transaction marked the modest beginnings of what proved to be a very long relationship with Barclays, which was Price's bank. They had security on quite a lot of the business when I bought it. Price had a bit of a land bank, but half a million pounds of debt, and I asked Barclays to give me 18 months to sort everything out, which they agreed to do.

I closed down the construction side of the company, which was the hugely risky area, and got a claims consultant in to look at the contracts. He was a really great guy. I paid him a percentage of what he could collect and he collected about £1.5 million of claims that weren't in the books.

I also analysed the accounts of the house building side of the company, and worked out that it predominantly made money out of inflation. If Price had had 100 plots in 1976, you had then built on them and sold them and then in 1980 you had tried to repurchase the land to go again, you might as well have sat on the land because the annual inflation rate over that period was 5%–6% or more. Price had plenty of options to buy land. I thought to myself, *why am I employing people to build houses with all the cyclical risk that involves?*

Cwmbran was one area where Price had an option to buy land. A bypass was built around the town and this isolated land on the north side of the town – this land turned out to be worth a lot of money. I decided that I didn't want to finance the building of houses there – I'd go to a national housebuilder like Bovis or Barratt and say, "Why don't I put the land into a joint venture with you? I don't want any monies for it now, but I'll get 22% of the house price when you sell it." So off I went and did a deal to provide the plots for 200 houses.

The result was that I closed the operating business within two years and had very few employees. We did no contracting or house building – we just had the land contracts earning 22% of the selling price of the house when completed.

That's when I learned to play golf! It was time well spent, because golf has been a lifelong pleasure.

This was money easily earned – you might say too easily. I didn't really have anything to do. I'd come back from the golf course at 4.00 pm, call the lawyers and they would say, "Plots 14, 17 and 18 have sold so that's £28,000 from each of them in the bank." By 1981, the business had about £3–4 million of cash.

However, Lesley was getting fed up with me being at home – because I'm pretty useless at home. I remember watching 'The Magic Roundabout' with the kids every afternoon. It was nice to be with the children, but following the fortunes of Dougal and Zebedee wasn't really my thing – I was more interested in the stock market. Increasingly, I found myself thinking, *this can't go on*. I was only 34 and sitting on a few million. In those days, £5 million was a lot of money; you could live on that for a long time. But I had no ambitions to join the rentier class. I wanted to build a business and I sensed a chance to do just that.

At this time, Britain was feeling the first impact of the Thatcher revolution. Many people today have the wrong idea about Thatcher – they just label her as a Conservative. Of course she led the party, but she was really a radical who overturned the post-war Establishment. The process of injecting dynamism into the British economy was painful – it had been declining for decades.

In early 1990, I was invited to lunch at 10 Downing Street with Mrs Thatcher. We had a wide-ranging discussion and I remember she came out with one particularly memorable line. We were talking about the fall of the Berlin Wall the previous year and its implications, particularly for the reunification of Germany – which she opposed. Having lived through the Second World War, she had a real fear of the size and power of a Germany at the heart of Europe – I think that's why she was a supporter of the European Union, but with serious reservations about its drift towards federalism. Our lunch ended when she had to leave for a vote in the House of Commons, and her parting shot was: "I like the Germans so much that I want two of them!" Unforgettable.

Unemployment shot up in the early eighties as overmanned companies, in both the public and private sectors, struggled to adjust to the government's monetarist policies. Companies had lived off a weak pound and high inflation for years – this allowed them to increase profits without having to do much to earn that growth – so they were shocked when the government declared war on inflation and jacked up interest rates. At the same time, the overthrow of the Shah of Iran triggered an upsurge in global oil prices – just when North Sea oil production was building up. As a result, the pound went through the roof, which made things even tougher for businesses, particularly for industrial firms. A deep recession ensued, starting in 1980.

Relatively few newcomer companies – today we'd call them disruptors – saw the early eighties slump as an opportunity. Hanson and BTR were the best-known. They were conglomerates controlling a vast empire with rigid financial controls. They grew fast by using their highly-rated shares to buy depressed companies at a fraction of underlying value. They then increased the earnings, which in turn boosted their share price and enabled them to make more acquisitions. It was a kind of Indian rope trick.

I had been watching Hanson and BTR, as well as Slater Walker, the outfit that in many respects was their forerunner as a financially-driven holding company. I had always had the idea that economic upturns start in a contra-cyclical way, in that assets become under-valued and therefore cheap. The pendulum always swings too far one way or the other in terms of under- or over-valuation, and the early eighties was a classic example of this fundamental fact of business life. The UK's industrial heartland was on its knees – the engineering sector in particular was hugely under-invested and de-rated by the stock market. I thought it would be a great time to buy some of these businesses, which were moribund in market capitalisation terms. Not because I wanted to asset-strip them, although that was a form of backstop, but to position them for an upturn when these assets were worth more.

To do this, I needed a public company vehicle, so that I could use the currency of its equity to make the acquisitions I wanted. I was a novice at this game, so I visited a few investment banks – merchant banks as they were then known – to tap into their merger and acquisition (M&A) expertise. I also put some feelers out in South Wales and looked at various companies. I found one in particular which looked a promising place to start; an aluminium die-casting business with a number of small non-ferrous brass foundries around the Caerphilly/Cardiff area. It was called W. Williams and Sons, and its market cap. had dwindled to £200,000.

But I knew little about the City and how the stock market really worked – I didn't even know any stockbrokers. However, I knew a man who did. He was the former assistant company secretary of London & Northern, whom I had met when I sold the plant hire business to them all those years before. His name was Brian McGowan.

I had first met Brian at a lunch at London's Savoy Hotel to celebrate L&N's acquisition of the plant hire business. I was invited because I had negotiated the deal, and Brian was there because he organised the Savoy lunches that L&N held after completing each acquisition. 'Lunch' was actually a misnomer – as I discovered, these events lasted all afternoon and ran into the evening, by which time most of the guests were much the worse for wear. On this occasion, a drunken brawl broke out.

That evening Brian and I, as the two young bag-carriers, sat on the side-lines of all this, chatting away and discussing how we would do things differently from L&N. When the fight broke out, we just looked at each other and said, almost in unison: "If we can't do better than this, we deserve to be shot!"

That was the start of a friendship which has now lasted more than 50 years. We are different characters and we complement each other; Brian always used to say that the main difference between us was, and still is, that I'm amazed we were so successful whereas he is merely surprised that it took so long. But we had the same sense of humour and ambition, our two eldest boys were about the same age and our families got on really well.

After the Savoy meeting, we continued to watch how Jock Mackenzie ran L&N, and we discussed things in greater detail, including what we might want to do in the future. Brian left L&N

in 1974 to run the acquisition team at shipping company P&O, but we continued to meet regularly. Then Brian decided to go to Hong Kong to work as finance director for the huge Malaysian-based holding company Sime Darby. He was there for six years and we kept in touch. We discussed doing something together and recognised our different strengths. Brian is very precise and organised, and he had the City experience I lacked. We didn't want to do a start-up. We both understood acquisitions, so the idea was to find a vehicle which we could develop.

In the early 1980s eventually I asked him: "How are you getting on out there?" He replied: "My wife wants to come back to England." So I went out to see him in early October 1981 and we met on his birthday, 3 October. I said: "Why don't we have a go at doing a Hanson Mark 2? If I can find a shell company, why don't you come in with me? We've both made some money, and we aren't going to put it all into our venture, but let's put some in and have a go."

Happily, Brian replied: "If we're ever going to do it, now's the time."

2

Williams

I flew back to the UK and a few weeks later, on 30 October, I called Brian in Hong Kong and told him: "I've found the right vehicle."

Brian replied: "That's great, where is it?" and I explained that it was in South Wales, to which his response was, "Bloody hell, I've never had a great deal of success with investments in Wales. Anyway, what is it?" It was a foundry. "A foundry? Terrific – they are all losing money!" said Brian.

"You haven't heard the best of it," I told him. "It's losing nearly £1 million a year. But it is cheap."

Brian flew back to the UK in early November and we looked at Williams together. It was in Barclays' recovery department. It had indeed lost almost £1 million the previous year and had net tangible assets of £2.1 million. The family who controlled it owned almost half the shares and were getting worried – I think they were quite frightened that they might lose all their money.

Brian was reluctant at first. In fact, after he looked at the balance sheet, he exclaimed: "Are you mad? Is this really what we want to buy?" I said: "Yes – there are plenty of assets there including a site in Caerphilly which is probably worth the market cap. We could sell that if we had to." Brian came round and we talked to Charterhouse, which was one of the investment banks I had been to see. They knew the company and told us it would be for sale. We negotiated, and one of the first things I learned was how duplicitous investment bankers are! They went behind our back and tried – but failed – to sell the company to someone else.

Once we had got through that nonsense, we faced another obstacle. The London Stock Exchange (LSE) rules, then as now, stipulated that if you bought 30% or more of a company's shares, then you had to bid for the rest. That was no use to Brian and me because we wanted Williams' stock market quote – its equity currency – to use in further acquisitions. Williams' stockbroker was Liddon and Co. in South Wales, and we said to them: "The trouble is that if we make a full bid for this business, we'll lose the quote. We want the quote but we also want control – it is no good us buying 10% and the family making a fortune off the back of us. So we want at least 60%."

Liddon said: "We'll go and talk to the LSE and see if they will make an exception in this case."

So off they went and in the end, the LSE said that we could buy 60% of the company and keep the stock market listing for the other 40%. That was pretty remarkable and would never happen today, with the inflexible regulation that now exists. All of this was purely on the basis that, without our bid, the business would probably have gone bust. We reached agreement with the family to buy 60% of Williams for £300,000 – I invested £200,000 and Brian put in £100,000.

I became chairman and he became chief executive, but we agreed that it was a partnership. Our respective titles reflected the fact that I was there to do the deals and Brian, who unlike me knew how everything worked in the City, was there for all the financial management. We didn't really have a finance director because we felt that we could do that ourselves – and for many years at Williams, we never had an FD.

This was a time before remuneration committees were independent of the executive. Brian and I decided that we should be paid the same amount, and since we were the remuneration committee, we fixed our own pay. Outrageous in this day and age, and since amounts did not have to be disclosed in the accounts, you might think that we would have paid ourselves excessive amounts – but in fact we thought our pay was a fair reflection of the time and effort we were putting in. When disclosure became mandatory, we were shocked to find out that compared to our contemporaries in other companies we were woefully underpaid. The newly-independent remuneration committee duly increased our compensation to our peers' level.

We could never go back to non-disclosure of pay, but in my opinion the way that benchmarking has ratcheted up rewards for executives is a classic case of the law of unintended consequences. The idea that disclosure moderates reward has proved false. Quite the contrary is, in fact, the norm.

We also established an important principle about succession. We had the same view about nepotism – we had seen too many family-controlled businesses come to grief because those running them had installed sons or daughters as successors – sons or daughters who weren't up to it. So we agreed from the outset that if either of us ever suggested that his children should come into the business, that would require the proposer to sell all his shares to the other partner. In the event, neither of us ever suggested that this should happen.

We sat down and studied Williams' portfolio and it was in really horrible shape. The main asset was the dilapidated, loss-making foundry in Caerphilly, which we thought we could eventually close and sell as a supermarket site. We asked Rapleys, the property agents, to value the factory. Jim Banks was their senior partner, and he became a lifelong friend.

The theoretical value of the site figured in every document we filed with the banks and the Stock Exchange – cash-flow forecasts, asset values, the lot – for the next three or four years. Eventually, it became insignificant in the context of Williams and we actually sold it about six years later for very little. But its notional value was absolutely vital for our survival in those first two or three years.

Williams' main customer was Girling, the automotive brakes arm of Lucas, which was then one of the UK's largest manufacturers of motor components. But Girling was under huge pressure at the time because it was sub-scale and so its volumes were down – hence Williams' dire performance. First, we had to stop the losses, so we did what you should do in these circumstances: we injected some cash while tightening up the working capital. We got through the stabilisation phase, which was the hardest part. But although the share price was holding up, it was not really going anywhere.

With Brian McGowan, in the early days with Williams

Then, out of the blue, I got a call from Bill Jamieson, who was the London-based City editor for Thomson Regional Newspapers (TRN). TRN owned a string of regional and local papers in the UK, and one of its flagships was the *Western Mail*, the Cardiff-based daily. Bill, who died in late 2020, was well-respected and his copy went to all the TRN papers in England and Wales, so anything he wrote was widely-read. I think Bill had been talking to our broker. He said: "I want to write an article about you. It will say that a Far Eastern investor and a British whiz kid are taking over this company, Williams, which is a stock to watch."

There was no market in our shares at the time, but after the story appeared in December 1981 and we completed the Williams deal, they took off. Our market capitalisation went from £500,000 to £3 million in no time. At the time, Williams actually wasn't worth £500,000! I said to Brian: "Christ – we've got to issue some shares and buy some businesses." We had a rights issue to take advantage of the share price rise and increase our firepower, modest as it was.

I also decided that I wanted to return to Derby – we'd had enough of living in South Wales. So in 1982, we set up a little office there while Brian remained in South Wales. After moving back, I started putting together the small team that has since been absolutely invaluable to me over the years.

First, I persuaded a bookkeeper–accountant to join me. Muriel Davies had been a wonderful support to me when I was turning round the business I bought from L&N, and she worked with me until her untimely death 10 years ago. Muriel looked after all my record-keeping and personal financial affairs, which are quite complex. She was meticulous in everything she did and her loss was terribly sad.

My daughter, Jennifer, stepped into the breach and together with Sue Dodd, my personal assistant, very rapidly picked up the pieces. Jen is one of the most organised people I know, and got everything under control. She has a very good degree from Edinburgh and met Gordon, her future husband, there. She spent some time working in financial public relations, but after about a year she phoned me to say that she was quitting. I asked why, and she was pretty honest: "Dad, I don't like telling people things I don't believe in." I thought to myself, *if that's the case then politics is out as well!* She then worked in fund management until their first child came along, and she and Gordon now live in Oxfordshire and London with their three children.

Kevin, my driver for over 30 years, shared so many great excursions and until his retirement in 2020 was almost part of the family. I employed him personally, and he made life so much easier. He could turn his hand to anything and hated doing nothing. He acted as my loader when I went shooting, helped in the garden and did a host of other things for us – in the last year, I have realised exactly how much. Now, I have to arrange for the car to be serviced and manage all sorts of other chores that Kevin did happily. I realise how spoilt I'd become!

I needed a PA when I moved back to Derby and Sue interviewed very well. She was a bright grammar school girl with a history of working for senior people in a number of businesses, including Rolls-Royce, so I offered her the job and she accepted. Little did I know then that she would become an integral part of my business success, not only at Williams but in all my directorships to this day.

Everyone who has had any dealings with Sue over the years knows the value that she adds to everything I do. She handles the diary, organises all my travel, protects me from people who want to waste my time and generally makes my life bearable. She also organises the events for the golfing group that I formed, the Mulligans, whose meetings have become a high point in so many people's golfing year. Having worked with me for so long, Sue knows all my contacts and can easily assess whether there is something I need to do immediately or if something can wait. Among my friends and my business colleagues, she is a legend.

Yet, this was very early days for Williams and it could still have gone *phut*, so Brian and I stepped up our search for similar kinds of businesses to bulk the company up both industrially and financially.

One of the first things I did after returning to Derby was talk to a few of my contacts in the Midlands about opportunities to acquire businesses with undervalued assets. One day, my personal bank manager called to say that there was a private company called Allison, a kind of mini-conglomerate; it was based in Hull, was in serious financial trouble and probably going into receivership. It was a mixture of BMW and Vauxhall car dealerships, a block-making plant, swimming pool installation and bits of quarry land, but it had over-extended through the management having taken too much cash out of the business.

The bank manager thought that the two BMW dealerships, in

Hull and Doncaster, would be of interest to us, and he arranged for me to meet the local representatives of the bank trying to sell the business, either pre-receivership or in administration. I met them in Nottingham and agreed to have a look at the business. I met the owners, a father and daughter, and that meeting went quite well – although it was apparent to me that they had virtually given up on any chance of rescuing the company.

We thought we could buy the business for a pound, but obviously we would have to take on all the external debt. We entered into a very cleverly-organised contract drawn up by our then-lawyer, Robin Geldard, which made the purchase conditional on the state of the company being no worse than we had been led to believe. Brian and I thought that this would be quite good for a first Williams deal, because we could sell the other pieces off and keep the BMW dealerships, which we reckoned would be quite profitable. We weren't concerned that they were service, not industrial, businesses – our focus was on the purchase price relative to the asset value.

I also had a conversation with a chap I knew, Bill Rhodes, who was an accountant by training and had sold a stake in a construction company where he had been finance director. Bill had made himself financially secure with that deal and was now looking for something else to do. Bill was a shrewd guy and I trusted him completely, so I knew he could be very helpful: if we bought the car dealerships, we would need someone to spend time making sure the management systems were all in place while thoroughly researching the industry.

I told Bill that we couldn't afford to pay him, but that he might enjoy the experience and happily he agreed to work with us. He became a great addition to the Williams board, and even bought and leased back a dealership property to help us with our cash flow – it was not a bad deal for him either, as he later sold the property back to us in exchange for Williams shares. He actually ran some of our businesses in the first few years, but eventually wanted less day-to-day involvement and so became a non-executive. He joined me on the board of Pendragon when it was floated and, since his real forte was everything to do with pension funds, he became chairman of the pension fund trustees. Later, he even gained an MBA with a thesis on the subject.

Getting to know the City

We started due diligence on the BMW dealerships and I went to Hull to have a look at the business there. I quickly discovered that the most valuable element was not the dealerships themselves, lucrative as those were, but their general manager (GM). His name was Trevor Finn and he was the youngest GM that BMW UK had ever had – he was only about 23 when I met him that day in Hull. Trevor was one of those immensely talented people who had somehow been missed by the education system. He had left school with no qualifications and started as an apprentice mechanic at a Co-Op garage in Hull. Allison had recruited him and he had been rapidly moved through the service and parts business to sales and recently to GM.

My first conversation with Trevor was naturally very cagey, as he had no idea if we were serious about wanting to buy the business. But I made a mental note to go straight back to him if we decided to proceed. Attractive as the BMW dealerships were, there was one apparently insurmountable problem: in all its agreements with dealers, BMW reserved the right to terminate a franchise on change of ownership. This became even more of an issue as we looked more closely at the other businesses in the group, since we found that they were clearly in a worse state than we had believed, and included unquantifiable environmental problems. We therefore informed the bank that we were no longer going to proceed with the deal. The company went into receivership. The family owners were furious with us, of course, because they had put some personal guarantees into the company. But there was no way that we could sensibly have proceeded on the original terms.

Spicer and Pegler were appointed as receivers, and I knew one of the partners there. I called him and said that we would like to buy the BMW dealerships. However, he didn't understand the problems of transferring the franchise and the block that BMW had on that. By now it was early July, and I rang Trevor Finn and arranged to go back to Hull to see him. This meeting was a lot more productive than our first – for me, it was an extraordinary learning experience.

When I arrived, Trevor was on the phone to a customer. He beckoned me into his office while he continued the call. The man on the phone was asking about delivery of the car he had ordered. He was very anxious, because he wanted the car to be delivered in August which was then the only month in the year when the UK registration plate changed. August was a massive month in the trade because so many people – like the customer on the phone – wanted to be among the first to get the new number plate.

Pecking order was very important. Outside the cities and the immediate south-east, in what people might call 'middle England', having the newest model of a car was a status symbol. Going to the golf club, showing you were the first person with the new year's model, was a big thing. People used to ring us up, saying they had to have their car before somebody else. Trevor had an expression: "You can't take your house to the restaurant." Which meant that if you were someone important in your community, you couldn't go out somewhere and say, "Look at my big house." But you could show off your car. And it helped to define you, your position in society.

Throughout the year, BMW operated a policy of keeping product in short supply, because this persuaded customers that there was always a waiting list and not only kept new car prices high, but residual values too. As a result, BMW and Mercedes Benz – who did the same thing – were the most profitable brands in the car retail business. The strategy of ensuring that demand always exceeded supply was felt most acutely in the run-up to the August peak.

That morning in Hull, Trevor was explaining to the concerned customer that, although his car was in production, August delivery could not be guaranteed because there was a huge problem with supply. He said that if the customer immediately ordered additional options, such as leather seats, then they could be factory-fitted and this would jump the queue and accelerate delivery. The customer promptly signed up for just about everything Trevor suggested, and Trevor promised to do his best to have the car delivered in August. As soon as he put down the phone, he got up from his desk and, with a twinkle in his eye, told me to follow him to the back of the dealership. There, 20 or 30 brand new cars were lined up, including the car for the customer, replete with all the extras!

That was the start of the teach-in Trevor gave me on the workings of the business. He told me about current industry trends and that what was becoming popular were cars with, in his words, "magic feet and a bidet" (this meant cruise control and a rear wash and wipe facility). He was also open about how they had recently made a serious mistake with a Hull business owner who was one of their biggest customers. His wife got a new car every year and always had leather seats, but this time they had ordered the wrong specification – it was the right colour but had plastic seats. She was just about to collect the car when they realised the error and rushed a staff member off to buy several aerosol cans of Pledge furniture polish, with which they sprayed all the seats. The polish had just dried when the woman arrived. She opened the driver's door and exclaimed: "Goodness, I love the smell of leather."

The most important lesson I learned from Trevor that day was that about 40% of all new BMWs were sold in August, and that the dealerships made roughly 90% of their annual profit that month. "So if you buy the two dealerships before the first of August, you will have a great start," Trevor said. I thanked him, left and rang Brian.

"I know it's a risk to buy the properties knowing BMW could veto the transfer of the franchise." I said, "But they would have a hell of a problem replacing the dealerships, especially with August coming along." Brian agreed and we offered the receiver around £300,000 for the dealerships together with a few other property assets. Spicer and Pegler were delighted because every other bidder, of which there were several, had made BMW's agreement to transfer the franchises a condition of their offer. We just gave the receiver a cheque. Our only condition was that completion had to take place before 31 July, and the receiver agreed.

BMW went wild. They hired transporters to take away all the stock that was legally still theirs and after several very angry phone calls, at very short notice we finally managed to arrange a meeting at their head office in Bracknell, Berkshire. I was up in Hull, so trekked back down, met Brian and went straight into the meeting. We put our cards on the table: we owned the premises and other assets, we would continue to service customers, BMW could pull the plug but their reputation in the Hull and Doncaster areas would be severely damaged and they had no time at all to get other representation before the peak month.

After several hours of threats and counter-threats, we came to an agreement of sorts: we would run the dealerships without the legal franchise for three months, and after that we would co-operate in the sale of the premises and the business to a third party. However, we hoped that we would persuade them at that point to give us the franchise. The low-loaders were turned around and I got back to my Hull hotel at 3.00 am. At 8.00 am, I met a smiling Trevor Finn at the dealership.

We put Trevor in charge of the dealerships and soon we all had plenty to smile about: that August of 1982, the two dealerships sold a record number of new cars. Cash was tight initially, because we had to finance the trade-ins that inevitably accompanied each transaction, but as we sold the glut of new cars, the money started to roll in. By the end of October, we had £400,000 in cash, so the dealerships had cost us minus £100,000.

We also spent that period demonstrating to BMW that we were fit and proper partners. In those days, BMW had a natural aversion to corporate owners, because individuals were always more willing to spend on premises and, quite frankly, to do as they were told. In a sense, the BMW network was a club, best suited to owners who relied on being part of the so-called family, whereas corporates like us were suspected of wanting higher returns on their capital and therefore less willing to invest in the dealership.

But in that three months, we did everything that BMW asked us to do. If they wanted us to change the showroom decoration, we did it. Our people turned up en masse at dealer meetings. We were all over them. In the end, they decided to grant us a contract on the two dealerships and they were highly profitable for more than 30 years in what became the Pendragon group.

Apart from the cash we generated from the dealerships, we also sold some of Allison's peripheral businesses and property. So by the time BMW confirmed our ownership of the dealerships, we had made three or four times our £300,000 outlay and we were more than ready for our next deal.

With Michael Heseltine

In my home city of Derby, there was a company called Ley's Foundries and Engineering. In its heyday (which had been some time ago), Ley's was the largest malleable foundry business in Europe and one of the first companies in Britain to make castings for the motor industry. Founded by Francis Ley in the 1880s, it had remained a family business ever since. It had also created a piece of sporting history. When he founded the company, Francis Ley adopted an American casting process and imported a number of engineers from the United States on short-term contracts to implement the process. The Americans got a bit homesick, so they started to play baseball on open land at the back of the Leys factory and turned the area into a baseball diamond. They went on to set up a national league in England, although this collapsed after they finished their work and returned home.

But they left a significant legacy, because at around the time they began to pitch and hit, Derby County football club was formed as an adjunct to the town cricket club and played on the cricketers' Racecourse ground. In 1888 the Football League was formed, with Derby one of its 12 founder members, and shortly afterwards County fell out with the cricket club and left the Racecourse. At this point, Francis Ley said to them: "Come and play at our baseball ground." And that's how the original Derby County football stadium got its name. County played there for more than a century before moving into Pride Park in 1997. I started going to watch them as a boy and later became a season ticket holder. I sit with Sir Ralph Robins, the great former Rolls-Royce chairman and chief executive, who is also a native of Derbyshire.

Derby County's new ground, Pride Park, is situated on a vast industrial and commercial site which was created thanks to an initiative by Michael Heseltine in the early 1990s. He came up with an idea to rejuvenate areas of deprivation in mainly Midlands and northern towns and cities, and called it City Challenge. It was a competition in which local authorities were asked to submit bids for a project in their area with the best ones being chosen by the government and receiving funding.

Derby City Council wanted to make a bid and they asked me to chair it on their behalf. On the east side of Derby there was a vast area of unused land. It had been a gas works, but all sorts of contamination rendered it unviable for development by the council because the reclamation costs that they would have to pay were greater than the commercial value. We assembled a team and devised a plan to use City Challenge money to reclaim the land, which we named Pride Park. Our design involved putting a huge bund right round the site, with a huge treatment works to capture the contaminated water run-off as it left the site.

Our bid was a winner and we then completed the civil engineering work. The site was ready to go when the UK economy took a downturn, causing companies' interest in locating on the site to completely dry up. Then I heard that the Prudential insurance group was going to start an online bank called Egg. I rang the chairman Peter Davis, whom I had dealt with when he was running Reed

International, and he told me that they were considering several sites – including Pride Park.

I immediately organised our team to love-bomb the Prudential and eventually we convinced them to choose us. Egg came and created several thousand jobs, and that encouraged other organisations to follow – including the football club. I was knighted in 1996 and, whilst you never know the background to such an honour, I think that my role in the Pride Park achievement was one of the reasons. In terms of investment and job creation, it was just about the most successful of the City Challenge schemes.

Under Brian Clough and Peter Taylor in the 1970s, Derby won the First Division (forerunner of the Premier League) and reached the semi-final of the European Cup (now the Champions

With the Hon. Sir Greg Knight MP at
Pride Park

League). Ley's Foundries and Engineering was less successful: by 1982, it was in deep trouble. The Leys were very much local industrial aristocracy – Francis Ley had been created baronet in 1905 and the company was now run by his great-grandson, Sir Ian, whose father, Sir Francis, was still alive. They were frightened that the company might not survive.

Nevertheless, Ley's was perfect for us: Williams probably had gearing of about 200% at the time we spotted it – and that was a generous number because our borrowings were real and the assets might not have been. Ley's had no borrowings and £10 million of real assets. We could get it for £3.5 million in cash, which would push up our borrowings to £5.5 million but increase our assets by a net £7 million. It would transform our balance sheet.

The key was to find the money. Brian knew and got on well with Oliver Brooks, P&O's finance director. They had a finance subsidiary called Twentieth Century Banking, which they had picked up when they bought the construction company Bovis. Twentieth Century had been in the banking sector lifeboat during the 1973 UK fringe banking crisis. Brian went to see Oliver and managed to persuade him and Twentieth Century to lend us the whole £3.5 million. He made it a condition that Brian and I each sign a personal guarantee of £1 million. Those guarantees stayed put for about four years before we removed them – by that time, we were quite a large public company and I think we just forgot about them.

Ley's was a stepping-stone: it got us recognised and gave us a bigger balance sheet. As with the Allison dealerships, by far the most valuable aspect of the acquisition was not the business but one of its managers – in this case, their head castings salesman, one Roger Carr. Roger was obviously a very bright man, very meticulous and knew the company inside out. As soon as we bought the company, he rang me and said: "I have produced a dossier on what we should do with this business."

Brian and I had a rough idea to close Ley's and use the cash we released in the process to make bigger and better deals. Roger was on the same page, but more sophisticated in his thinking about how to go about it, and we decided to phase the shutdown over the next 18 months. We cut the cost base, but the business was still haemorrhaging cash. It had assets literally hanging around all over the place – in floorspace terms, it still had the largest foundry in Europe occupying almost a square mile, with its own internal railway track. This was not being used, so we started lifting all the rails and putting them into the cupola to provide raw material for the castings. The operation was eating itself, but still it was not profitable.

One of the main reasons for the continuing losses was the terms on which Ley's was trading with British Leyland (BL), the government-controlled vehicles giant, which was one of its two largest customers (the other being the tractor maker Massey Ferguson). While BL had been losing market share for years, despite its mounting problems it was still the predominant customer for many British motor component firms, which would bend over backwards to accede to its demands, as Ley's had always done.

The control that BL exerted over its suppliers stemmed partly from the fact that it usually owned the tooling for components, so it was at liberty to move the work around, using different suppliers depending on who was the cheapest. This was fairly common practice in the British motor industry and gave the vehicle makers, the OEMs (original equipment manufacturers), the whip hand over their suppliers in any price negotiation. It also made them notoriously bad customers, but the suppliers had to like it or lump it.

Ley's was no different, with one important exception. In the case of one particular casting for the Mini, we – not BL – owned the patterns for tooling and production. The current Mini model was due to be replaced in 18 months and we were called to a meeting at BL's main factory, Longbridge in Birmingham, to discuss the changeover. At the meeting, BL told us we had to cut the price of the castings by 20% if we wanted to supply the new model. We refused and told them that we would halt production immediately. They replied that this was fine and demanded that we sell them back the patterns, whereupon they would re-source. But we said: "No – we aren't going to do that, either. We will put a hammer through the patterns unless you give us a price increase of 50%, and if you do that, we'll produce all the castings you need until the current model runs out."

This was Roger's strategy – it was David versus Goliath stuff. Initially, BL were apoplectic – I assume no-one had stood up to them like this before, certainly not a minnow like us. They told us that, if we destroyed the patterns, we would close their production line. Our response was, "That's your problem – you have been screwing us on price over the years." Then they said: "You will never do business with us again" – and I retorted: "That is the best thing I have heard today!"

In the end, they had to knuckle under and so we made enough money to close the plant down and pay off the workers in full. All our equipment was antiquated and we sold it to Jon Moulton, who had started Schroder Ventures as the venture capital arm of Schroders investment bank. We had bought a few other small companies by then and sold Schroders a package of businesses in a deal we code-named Flush, as in With Cash – not Down the Plughole.

The one big attribute that Ley's had was a huge surplus in its pension fund. Unlikely as it sounds in today's environment, with many company funds in deep deficit and final salary pension schemes almost extinct, at that time and for a good many years afterwards, many companies had substantial unused pension fund surpluses. During 1983, we used the money from the pension fund surplus and the Schroders sale to buy additional smaller companies for cash. In the process, we made some money but we also took on quite a lot of debt, because some of the businesses were a bit flaky.

Shortly after the Ley's acquisition, Williams' shares hit a 10-year high of 56.5 pence and went on rising thereafter. By April 1984 they were well above one pound, so we did a rights issue, our first, at 117 pence which raised £2.8 million and put us in a position to do a bigger deal. A number of long-term investors came on board at that point, which was very important because they were ready to support our expansion. And eight months later, we got our big breakthrough – the acquisition that really made Williams.

Investiture at Buckingham Palace with Edward, Tim and Jen

3

Breakthrough

I was always an avid reader of the *Investor's Chronicle* – it had fantastic articles on small companies. On Boxing Day 1984, I was hiding from the kids somewhere and I picked up the Christmas edition of the *IC*.

They had written a piece about a company called J. and H. B. Jackson. It was a strange business, with quite a big forgings operation in the UK and a little plastics operation in the US making cups for Holy Communion. But it was the balance sheet dimension that really grabbed me. Williams at that stage had a market capitalisation of about £14 million, assets of £10 million and net debt about £11 million; Jackson was the opposite – it had assets of £26 million and net cash of £11 million, yet its market capitalisation was slightly less than ours. I thought, *if we can get hold of this business, we will double our market cap., have assets of £30 million and wipe out our borrowings.*

As our share price showed, we had done well at Williams. We had established a reputation for transforming small, struggling businesses. But the cost of that progress in terms of our debt level had been high, and the assets we had accumulated were modest. As a result, we now faced a fairly stark choice: either spend our careers operating at a relatively low level by getting rubbish to run well, or make a leap to faster growth by buying a substantial, decent company and using that as a springboard into the higher-quality league. The latter was by far the more exciting alternative, but with our existing borrowings, if the slightest thing went wrong after such an acquisition, then we would be blown away.

That's what made Jackson so attractive. I said to Brian, "I'm sure that other people have looked at this but we ought to have a go at trying to buy it." We were very thorough: we prepared a 46-page analysis explaining why Jackson made such good sense for Williams and then we had to find a merchant bank and a stockbroker to advise us on the bid.

Brian had a couple of contacts. One was at Barings, so we went to see them. Their office was in a modern, high-rise building in Bishopsgate, near Liverpool Street station. We went up to the top floor and were given lunch, and set out what we were trying to do. And they absolutely looked down their noses at us – I assume it wasn't because of our table manners –were really snobby and essentially said, "You are really much too small for us to advise. Come back when you are four times larger and we might consider acting for you." We came out utterly humiliated. I have to admit that, when Barings went bust about 10 years later, I felt a little bit of *schadenfreude*.

Having exited Barings with our tail between our legs, that same week Brian got us in to see Schroders, who were on the other side of the City from Barings, at the top of Cheapside near St. Paul's Cathedral. When you entered the building, you were confronted by a huge clock, known as the Schroders clock, which showed the times in all their offices around the globe. Schroders was a historic name but it had come down in the world recently, suffering a slump in its market cap. to around £30 million.

Brian's contact was Win Bischoff, one of their top bankers who had just been brought back to London from Hong Kong by the Schroder family, in a bid to revive their franchise. Win and Brian had been in Hong Kong at almost exactly the same time and left almost simultaneously, and they had got to know each other really well. Win had come back to London as about number six in the corporate finance department, and within a year Schroders had removed the five people above him so that he suddenly became the department's head.

Schroders was losing blue-chip clients hand over fist to fast-rising rivals like Morgan Grenfell. Win was determined to stop this decline and to bring in new business. So, our reception could not have been more different from what we had encountered a few days earlier at Barings, with Win very welcoming and pleasant. I heard later that, after we had left, they had quite a heated internal debate about whether they should take us on or not. Apparently Win fought our corner and said, "Look, I know Brian from Hong Kong and although we don't know Nigel, we should take a punt on them." So they agreed to act for us on Jackson, and that was the start of a long and mutually rewarding relationship.

Win went on to have a stellar career in London: he became chairman of Schroders and in 2000 the investment banking business was bought by Citigroup for about £1.3 billion. He also ran Citigroup for a period in New York before becoming chairman of Lloyds Bank. He was very brave in taking us on in 1985. We were absolutely tiny then. But Schroders needed clients at the time; a fund manager friend of Brian's told him that we must have been their first new client for about 10 years.

The main person who looked after us there over the years was David Challen. David was highly intellectual and I credit him with always keeping our feet on the ground. That was important in the late 1980s and 1990s, after Williams had become a large and successful company, because people in the UK market would come up with all sorts of bizarre M&A ideas – one of the craziest was when Saatchi and Saatchi, the advertising group, considered bidding for Midland Bank.

David made sure that we didn't do anything silly, and he was a genuine adviser. So many investment banks will try to persuade you to do things because that earns them fees; then if it goes wrong, it's nothing to do with them. Schroders weren't like that – David and his team actually gave us more advice on why we shouldn't do something than why we should. Brian used to negotiate the fees with David and I don't think they ever had a disagreement. On one of our early deals, Brian asked him what fee he was proposing to charge if we failed with our bid and David – who had a very dry sense of humour – said: "I've seen your cash flow and I don't think you could pay us one."

Along with David, we had a succession of people working with us over the years, and they were all first-rate – the late Mark Warham, Andrew Shaw, Philip-Robert Tissot, Robert Swannell. Unlike some companies, we didn't use different banks for different deals: we were almost monogamous. The only time we didn't go with Schroders was when we bid for Racal in 1991 and that was because they were conflicted. I think not having them was one of the reasons we lost the bid.

We also had to find a London-based stockbroker, because Lyddon only operated in Wales. Slaughter & May were our main lawyers but we also regularly used our original Welsh lawyers, Edwards Geldard, on small transactions and they gave us an introduction to de Zoete & Bevan, one of the foremost City brokers. These were the days before Big Bang in 1987, when your broker would ring up a top fund manager and tell them, "You've got to buy these shares – and by the way, I've bought them for you already!" De Zoete had a partner called Johnny Townsend who took us on, and he promoted Williams until he left what had become Barclays de Zoete Wedd – BZW, the investment bank that Barclays created after Big Bang. He did a tremendous job for us. After him, Nick Brigstocke and Chris Chambers acted for us and acted for us very well. Nick wasn't as well-known as one or two of the other corporate broking stars, but he was up there with them, trusted by both companies and investors and giving first-class advice.

We were very fortunate with our advisers at Williams. We made some mistakes, but we always got balanced advice. Slaughters were also very good: Tim Freshwater looked after us with Frances Murphy, who died recently. That was very sad, as she was a great personal friend in the end. So we always had those three pillars of advisers, who were very good and blue chip. It is much harder to get that today: you often wonder which side the big American banks are on. As a result, I don't have the same confidence in advisers that I had years ago. Fortunately, I've accumulated a lot of experience – but it's different for the younger generation of chairs and chief executives. If you do a deal for the wrong reasons or at the wrong price, your company can get into a lot of trouble.

Back to Jackson. With our advisory team on board, Brian and I went to see Philip White, the Jackson chairman. He was based in a scrap yard in Coventry but, incongruously, his office contained huge Reuters screens – Jackson was boosting its profits by dealing in Canadian government bonds. White owned about 20% of the company and was moving to the Isle of Man, where he had bought a farm, as a tax exile. We suggested that a share swap would give Jackson a really good premium. But he told us: "You are about the four-hundredth people to come here because you want to get hold of my company, but I enjoy what I'm doing, so get lost." Except he put it a bit more bluntly. And subsequently his banking adviser, Barings, were very snooty and told him not to touch our shares with a barge pole. A few days after our meeting, White rang me and said: "We don't want your rubbish, over-valued paper."

Brian and I considered the situation. We thought, *if we bid for this company then our share price will probably take off because people will see that this would be a great deal for Williams.* Our debt would be cancelled out by their cash, and we'd have a larger, cleaner balance sheet. We refused to take no for an answer but we realised that, to get Jackson, we would have to do something we had never done before and make a hostile bid. On 24 March 1985, we put a formal offer on the table, offering £24 million in shares. They immediately rejected it.

The M&A world then was very different – and much more interesting – than it is now, when there are hardly any hostile bids. Yes, there are activists trying to get boards to break up companies and predators will frequently try to bear-hug and pressure boards into submission. But this stuff is a long way from the all-out takeover battles that you got regularly in the 1980s and 1990s.

This one played out very well for us because our bid had exactly the effect on our share price that we had anticipated. Our investors worked out very quickly that if we won, we would double our market cap. and eliminate our debt, making Williams a much more attractive company. So our share price took off, creating a virtuous circle where the value of our offer increased. That pulled up the price of Jackson shares, but we benefited from that because everyone could see that they were now following the value of the Williams offer.

We knew that White was no fool and he could see what was happening. I kept my lines of communication with him open, and pointed out how much value he had gained from the offer. I also reminded him of the downside: if we failed, then Jackson shares would slump and he and his shareholders would lose out in a big way. Barings could see which way the wind was blowing. We knew they were scouring the City for a white knight to counter-bid, but there wasn't one.

White was now in the Isle of Man, so Brian and I took a plane from Blackpool or somewhere to see him. It was clear to all of us that the share price appreciation meant it was impossible for him to continue to say no. White conceded and said that he would recommend our bid as long as we added a cash alternative, which we did. Schroders underwrote it, but most shareholders took our paper because they could see that its post-takeover value would almost certainly increase. So we were successful, despite having had to make an aggressive bid. It turned out to be the only hostile battle that Williams ever won, for reasons I will come to later.

We completed the main element of the integration – merging their cash with our overdraft – in about five minutes: it was the fastest integration we ever did. Buying Jackson was every bit as important as we thought it would be. Not only did it transform our balance sheet and double our size, but it also took us up-market. Jackson had an aerospace business making sophisticated aluminium forgings and, for a supplier, aerospace was much more attractive than automotive or other more basic industries. That's one fact of industrial life that hasn't changed in 40 years. The technology requirements of aerospace meant that the margins were infinitely superior to those in other engineering segments.

The Jackson takeover was crucial for another reason, too. Momentum is critical when you are trying to build a group, as we were. If we'd lost Jackson, it would have been a serious setback: our growth would have stalled, we would have remained saddled with onerous debt and above all, we would have suffered a sharp reverse in the eyes of investors and the City. Confidence in us would have been fractured and we would have been lumped into the 'wannabe' small cap. category. Of course, we would have bounced back, but the road would have been longer and harder. Instead, we were now, rightly, viewed as a winner with a strong springboard to further growth through bigger deals.

Jackson exemplified how Brian and I worked together. I had spotted the opportunity, then we brought our negotiating skills to bear and Brian's City knowhow enabled us to execute the deal. With his background, Brian could talk the City's language; he knew how to tell the story that would turn people on to our idea and he could work out how we were going to fund the acquisition.

Nick Brigstocke of BZW characterised the two of us as having "sharp business acumen, integrity and a single-minded determination to achieve the goals that they set themselves. They did not suffer fools gladly, but they were always rational, prepared to listen to advice and act upon it decisively if they accepted it. They made business enjoyable and their enthusiasm rubbed off on all those around them."

Our philosophy from the start of Williams was to build an asset base from which we could grow by acquiring more assets. We weren't interested in earnings per share: the big question for us was whether we could bulk up in terms of size and quality of real assets. That made us different from the other conglomerates like BTR, which emphasised profit and earnings per share – of course we wanted to grow profits, but for us the asset base came first.

So we continued to search for companies with undervalued assets. Part of our skill lay in deciding what not to buy. At one stage, we looked at the building products and engineering company Turner & Newall, which superficially fitted our main criterion: it had some solid assets priced by the market at a huge discount. But there was a good reason for that undervaluation – the company also had large historic asbestos liabilities, so we left it well alone. Years later, those liabilities caused a crisis at the American company that did take it over.

Some of our prime targets were businesses in really good niches where the competition wasn't huge, thus providing a large share of a small but lucrative market with high barriers to entry. If you look at the Williams companies, the most successful were those that fitted that description. They were great businesses because, although there was established competition, the cost to a prospective new entrant was so huge that no-one bothered, because the market simply wasn't big enough to justify the investment required. The first one like this was Rawlplug, which we bought from Burmah Castrol, the oil products group.

Rawlplug was a classic case of a really good niche business: it had a proprietary product (the small plastic fittings that hold screws in place) with a large share of a small market. The big multinationals weren't interested in entering that market – they had the resources to do so, of course, but it was too small for them, and it would have taken them years to create a business which could compete with the market leader. Rawlplug only had one main competitor, which was a privately-owned business called Plasplugs. That all demonstrated to us that you could develop the brand and grow the market without being attacked by a larger competitor. So, you could get a bigger profit margin. Crucially, you had power over the big retailers: they dominated most suppliers but they had to stock your brand because you were the leader.

What we also developed over this period was a comprehensive integration process to improve the businesses that we bought, which was headed by Roger and eventually became known as the special operations unit. We were buying businesses that had been under-managed, either because the company as a whole was not well run or because it was a peripheral subsidiary of a big group. A lot of people buy companies and let the management carry on doing what they have been doing, but we believed, basically, in shock and awe.

Roger's integration process was very effective – simple and systematic. When we were buying the business concerned, we did our own assessment of how we could improve the profitability and so on. Then, as soon as we completed the transaction, we gave the plan to the incumbent management and asked them to tell us where we were wrong.

This approach achieved two things: first it validated or invalidated our ideas, and secondly it told us an awful lot about the management. And that management fell into a number of categories. There were the people who would agree with you regardless, because they thought that was the way to keep their jobs; the ones who violently disagreed with you and left; and the really good ones who said, "You're right, but here is how you could do this" or "You don't understand the market because if you do this, you'll affect that." So at the end of that two- or three-month process, you really understood what was happening in the business. Then we could start the profit improvement plan.

During this period, we would send people into the business and look at the amount of stuff the managers had on their desks. We wanted to make a bit of a show, so we put our team into a small fleet of black BMWs and had them arrive en masse at the newly-acquired company. It was all a bit theatrical, but it made the point that there was new ownership, that things were going to change. Of course, the media loved it and presented it as Williams sending in the axemen to slash costs.

Cost reduction was part of what the integration team did, but there was a lot more to it than that. Michael Harper, who became one of our most important executives after he joined Williams in 1988, later described them as "pretty tough: they made it clear that their role in any business was very short-term, and they didn't give a stuff what people thought of them. as long as they fulfilled their remit. But they did an extraordinarily good job in the early days of Williams when it was buying businesses, tightening them up, investing in them and generally smartening them up."

Many acquirers only put in accountants – we had them too, but we also sent in people who were used to reorganising factories, others who were good in product improvement and short-cycle manufacturing. We had all of these skills and we could bring them to bear. So we made sure that we didn't take the existing management's eyes off the day-to-day business while we did all the work in terms of improving the operations, and then there was almost a ceremony of handing the business back to the management. It worked very well and Roger was very, very good at leading that. He was brilliant at taking cost out of a business and reorganising it, streamlining it.

After Jackson and Rawlplug we were very confident; we had a company that had grown strongly in a short space of time, and we had good support from our investors. We continued to look for companies which we thought were undervalued, and we spotted one in the shape of McKechnie, a long-established plastics and engineering components business which – like many such businesses in the mid-1980s – had been de-rated by the stock market. We bought a stake in it and then went to see its chief executive, a guy called Jim Butler. He was rather a patrician and seemed to regard our approach as an insult – indeed, he was outraged by it. It was obvious that we would have to go hostile, so we did. It was an opportunistic bid for a hugely undervalued company.

Williams' market cap. was about £90 million and McKechnie's was bigger – but the business was nowhere near as highly-rated. We made a paper bid worth £144 million and they were very much on the back foot. They countered with what was really a poison pill defence, by bidding for a smaller building products company called Newman Tonks. We had no interest in Tonks, so we made our offer contingent on McKechnie shareholders opposing the Tonks bid. We also did something that was pretty rare in those days, and told the market we would not increase our first offer because we believed it fully valued McKechnie and we would not overpay. The convention was that the first bid was always raised later in the battle, at least once and sometimes more. That was why the takeover panel operated a 60-day timetable for bids, but with McKechnie we set the deadline for acceptance much earlier.

In the end we lost by about 2%. McKechnie's Tonks bid never went through and years later, McKechnie was taken over by Melrose, whose philosophy of 'buying, improving and selling' businesses was similar to ours. I think several factors contributed to our failure. For one, it was a lesson to us about managing shareholders' expectations, about the relevance of overlap between shareholder registers – in this case, very few McKechnie investors had shares in Williams, and vice versa – and about how fund managers' perspectives were very different to our own view of a situation. To us, McKechnie was going nowhere and we aimed to persuade shareholders that our management was better than theirs. On top of that, we may also have been a victim of timing. Almost simultaneously, the Tomkins mini-conglomerate that Greg Hutchings had founded shortly after we set up Williams had narrowly won a bid for another undervalued Midlands engineer, Pegler-Hattersley. There was a sense in the City that a group of young Turks was laying siege to older, longer-established businesses, and we may have caught some backlash from that.

McKechnie was the first of a number of hostile bids that we lost over the years. Hostile bids were a kind of game, and you were expected to play by the rules. One of them was the need to be very aggressive and, despite appearances at times, we weren't by nature aggressive – ambitious and determined to grow through acquisition, but not out-and-out aggressive. You might say that we never learned to play the game, but in every case, our targets were underperforming businesses where, after thorough and totally objective analysis, we believed our management skills could increase value for all shareholders – but not at any price.

In several instances, including McKechnie, we would almost certainly have won if we had been prepared to offer more, but we were always extremely self-disciplined and we never paid more than we thought our target was worth. Our fundamental belief was that the quickest way to erode our own shareholders' value – and the trust that they put in us – was to overpay for acquisitions. That wasn't because we had a purist, arrogant, holier-than-thou approach. Quite the opposite: we knew that overpayment was a primrose path on which many other companies came to grief. Later in my career, I was asked to become chairman of some of these casualties and to sort out the mess that a bad, over-priced takeover had caused.

At Williams, we were always looking for value and we certainly felt we could pay up – we weren't trying to buy businesses on the cheap – but when you get down to it, that was the problem for us with hostile bids: you never know exactly what you are buying. You can't do any due diligence before the deal, and secondly, you know that the incumbent management are going to push value as far as they can, either by putting out an extreme profit forecast or doing something else to inflate the price that you are going to pay. That's why we felt much more at home with agreed bids. We could always do due diligence with a friendly deal, and as a result we were often prepared to pay a bit more than we originally offered, because we had got inside the business and understood it better.

We bounced back from McKechnie with a series of agreed bids of which by far the largest and the most significant was Duport, which had been a major iron and steel manufacturer before the industry was re-nationalised by the 1960s Labour government. It had morphed into an odd sort of conglomerate, with lots of niche businesses including consumer brands such as ViSpring beds and Swish shower curtain tracks.

Duport's chief executive was a guy called Jack Russell, who was a typical West Midlands industrial manager. I went to see him and unexpectedly furthered my education in management psychology. Russell was initially very opposed to any deal, but in the course of our discussions he introduced me to something which I never forgot.

He said in his strong Birmingham accent: "I operate on the five principles." I of course asked him what those principles were. And he held up his hand and, counting off on his fingers, said: "What's In

It For Me?" It's not exactly what they teach you in business school, but the 'social issues', as they are more delicately called, make or mar more deals than any grand corporate strategy.

Duport's finance director was dead-set against the deal and so were the non-executive directors. But I got on quite well with Russell. I assured him that we would offer a fair price for the business and that his own package and pension would be excellent, and we got the deal agreed. We paid about £80 million in shares and signed the deal on 12 May 1986.

Before completion, Schroders advised us to do some due diligence on Duport's pension fund, because they had a huge number of former employees dating back to the steel days and we didn't know the precise figures. But I said: "Don't look at the pension fund – I don't want that raising." We were still negotiating on price at that stage, and I told Schroders that I suspected they were down to roughly a tenth of the number of employees they used to have.

In the twenty-first century world of the UK Pensions Regulator and big pension fund deficits, that would have been a huge red flag, but at that time – as was the case on a smaller scale with Jackson – it was much more likely to mean that the fund had a hidden surplus. Early leavers were a benefit to a pension fund because their pay-out was very poor, so when you had as many as Duport did, you had a once-big fund which had become much smaller.

The first thing I did after we completed was to look at the pension fund. Brian and I suspected that it had a large surplus – by which we meant about £5 million. We discovered that they had not had a proper actuarial valuation for about eight years, so we did one and it revealed that they actually had a colossal surplus - about £60–70 million. So we effectively got the company for nothing.

We discussed how to use this windfall, and decided that first we should see about looking after the Duport pensioners. So we hired advisers to explain the maximum the law allowed us to do. There were a number of improvements that we put in place for the pensioners, but one of the most important was to retrospectively inflation-proof their pensions from the date they had retired. Inflation in the 1970s had been horrendous – it peaked at more than 24% in 1975 – so by the 1980s, the pensioners' real income was being badly squeezed.

The uplift they now received was in some cases enormous: one manager who had retired in 1971 on a pension of about £3,000 a year was now in his eighties and, because of all the inflation, that value was badly eroded. Because of what we did, his annual pension increased almost 12-fold to £35,000. Brian told the story to his father, who said: "That was really mean of you – you probably gave him a heart attack!" There was still a large amount of the surplus remaining after we had taken care of the pensioners, and that had a big benefit for Williams.

Pension funding used to go in cycles – you had cycles of over-funding and under-funding because the reaction to under-funding was to over-fund, and that is what happened in the Eighties. Then, because of the over-funding situation, people started to take pension fund holidays – unheard of now. I don't know whether you would get that cyclicality any more, because so many funds have been closed. But at the time, because of its very strong financial position, the Duport pension fund became the pension fund of Williams. We never took any money out of the fund, but what we did was pack all our other pension funds into it and enjoy the surplus. We were still taking a holiday in 2000, when the contribution we were saving was something like £20 million a year.

The Duport deal immediately boosted our market cap. and by June we were valued at more than £240 million. It also set us thinking about buying more niche, "orphan" brands. Having acquired Rawlplug and Swish, we were particularly interested in the building and consumer area. But we hadn't lost our taste for hostile bids if we felt the prospective prize was worth the time and trouble involved – and we had identified a new target.

4

Growth

Norcros was a building products manufacturer whose share price had stagnated because of lacklustre results. We bought a small stake and approached them for an agreed deal but were rebuffed, so we launched an aggressive all-share bid which valued them at just over £540 million, by far the largest acquisition we had attempted.

As with McKechnie, we had a very good idea what Norcros was worth and we were determined not to overpay. So we decided not to increase the bid and ran a shortened timetable. And once again, we fell short by about 2%; we got acceptances accounting for 48% of their shares.

This time, we lost for different reasons. One big factor was a simple mistake: one of their investors, Save & Prosper, which owned 3%, meant to accept our offer but filled in the form incorrectly and wasn't counted in with our votes. Without that error, we would have won.

But we also fell victim to the 'anything goes' attitude to takeover battles at that time. For instance, it was permissible for the share prices of defending companies to be supported by advisers, and Charterhouse, which was advising Norcros, bought a stake in the company, which helped to underpin its price. The main restriction on such activity was that support buyers had to finance the share purchases themselves – companies were not allowed to pay the institution or institutions involved, because that was tantamount to buying your own shares, which was forbidden by the takeover code.

In some takeover bids, one side or the other, or both, sailed close to the wind – and this trend culminated in the Guinness scandal which led to much tougher takeover regulation. The benefit for the adviser of a successful defence was that they retained a client, and Charterhouse duly received a very large fee from Norcros for helping to defeat us.

Despite our disappointment, Brian and I were determined not to let the defeat undermine our momentum. Our pick-me-up started the moment we heard that we had lost. We were with our advisers at BZW's office in the City when the news came through, and someone asked us what we were going to do now. And Brian said: "Open a bottle of champagne!" We immediately invited all the advisers to El Vino's, the famous wine bar in Fleet Street, and had a very enjoyable evening. It was important to restore the team's morale. We even sent Norcros a bottle with our congratulations – needless to say, we never got a thank you note.

Schroders' board room with Andrew Shaw, David Challen and David Porter of BZW

Once again, we bounced straight back from the Norcros reverse with one of the best deals that we ever did. It wasn't just that the deal was excellent in itself, but it opened up further value creation opportunities, which we were able to capitalise on over several years.

Reed International, the paper, packaging and publishing group, had decided to focus on specialist publishing and was selling non-core businesses (today Reed has evolved into RELX, the former Reed Elsevier). One of these units was its paints and DIY arm, which was a very good business because it had a number of well-known brands in the UK and North America. In the UK, there was Crown paints, which was number two to ICI's Dulux, and some very nice niche products such as Polycell. Everyone in the British DIY industry used Polycell for filling cracks, and Reed also had some decent businesses in continental Europe. Still more interesting was Reed's American paints portfolio, which contained leading 'regional' brands – Frazee down the US west coast, Parker in Tacoma near Seattle, Kwal Howells in Denver and Salt Lake City and General Paint in Vancouver.

The American businesses were very different from Crown, whose main customers were B&Q and the other big chains of retailing 'sheds'. As number two in a low-growth and price-competitive market, Crown had operating margins of about 6%, whereas the American businesses were making about 10%. They were vertically integrated, so they all had a paint manufacturing operation and 'decorator' paint stores, predominantly for small contractors who would come in each morning to get their paint mixed, have a coffee and then set off for the day's work. On the west coast, we had about 100 stores all the way down from Vancouver to San Diego with these different brands, all of them very well known in their region. They were extremely profitable.

We heard in the market that Reed was lining up a management buy-out (MBO) of these businesses. Reed's chairman and former chief executive, Leslie Carpenter, was heavily backing the MBO plan. So we approached Peter (later Sir Peter) Davis, Carpenter's successor as CEO, who ensured that we had a level playing-field. He was doing the right thing by his shareholders because that was the way to maximise Reed's proceeds. Eventually, we won the auction with a bid of £285 million. Crown came with some cash on its balance sheet, which reduced our net outlay to about £250 million, but it was still quite a mouthful for us, three times the size of Duport and by far our largest acquisition to date.

This was in June 1987. Four months later, on 19 October, the stock market crashed on Black Monday – the US Dow Jones Industrial Average plummeted almost 23% in a day, which was its biggest percentage drop since the Great Crash of 1929, and London's FTSE 100 fell 11%. Williams shares withstood the slump relatively well, but nonetheless we were hit, along with everyone else.

The crash couldn't have come at a worse time for us because we had identified an opportunity to transform Crown's performance through a second paints acquisition. There were three main players in the UK market, and as the number two to Dulux, who had the prized leadership position, we were not in a position to set the price. Crown was always concerned whether Dulux would be strong enough with retailers, because as number two it had to come in below them on price: like any market, you hope the leader will be tough on pricing and then you can still make a decent return underneath them.

What made the UK market particularly tough – and was restricting Crown's margins – was the presence of a very effective third player, Berger. Berger was owned by the German chemicals giant Hoechst and was an obvious target for us after acquiring Crown. There were no great competition issues because Dulux had such a big market share. Berger also had a presence in Asia-Pacific, based in Australia.

Hoechst were a client of Schroders and we heard from Mark Warham that they were prepared to sell Berger. Mark introduced us to the people at Berger and we were also able to look at the other, larger part of Hoechst's paints business, which was a very, very nice company in Portugal called Robbialac. On top of that, they owned Cuprinol wood preserver, which was a really fine business. The only major competitor in its niche was Ronseal, and the segment was effectively a duopoly. For years, ICI had tried to get into the wood care market and had failed because Cuprinol and Ronseal had invested a lot in marketing and had such strong positions. So this was a really attractive opportunity.

We agreed to pay £133 million for the whole paints business. The catch was that, having just made the big cash acquisition from Reed, we had to raise money in the market in order to fund most of the purchase price. The stock market was still reeling from the aftershock of Black Monday, and when we told BZW that we wanted to get about £100 million through a shares issue, they said there was no way that could be done in the current market. This was a real blow. We had a contingency plan for Crown if we didn't buy Berger, which was to sell the British business on to a continental European company or to Courtaulds, which had a small UK household paints operation, and to keep the US paint brands and Polycell. But the Berger deal was much better.

At this point, the trust that we had built up with our leading investors was crucial. We decided on an innovative approach: we would go to our five largest shareholders, make them insiders to the Berger deal and ask them each to agree to underwrite £20 million of the issue. If we could persuade them to do that, we knew that other institutions would come in since they would not be worried about being left with depreciating shares.

Initially, we considered issuing convertible loan stock rather than shares, but we dropped that idea after the first fund manager we approached told us that, if he wanted loan stock, he would buy government securities. He committed to take 20% of a straight equity issue, and so did three of the other four top investors. We gave all existing shareholders 'clawback' rights, which meant that they could take shares previously allocated to new investors so that their holdings would not be diluted by the new issue. Clawback was an article of faith in the City, and you breached it at your peril.

The rights issue was a success and Williams' share price actually rose after it, which was amazing in the face of a bear market. We completed the Berger deal, then sold their Asia-Pac operation to

ICI for £52 million. ICI was reluctant to meet our asking price at first, but soon changed their mind when we let them know that a US company was ready to pay up for the business.

That disposal reduced our net outlay to £81 million, and we brought it down further by selling other small Berger operations. On top of that, long before the Berger opportunity arose, we had taken a 5% stake in the British own-label paint and decorative products company A. G. Stanley. Berger owned 20% of Stanley, so we combined the stakes and, when the DIY group Ward White bid for Stanley in June 1988, we accepted the offer and realised £33 million for our shares. In less than six months, we recouped £110 million of the £133 million Berger purchase price.

Our general buying and selling of companies at this stage was pretty frenetic. I led on the big deals, but we were very fortunate to have two individuals who did all the hard graft in making these transactions happen: Tim Allen and Tim Park, who dealt with the banks, the lawyers and led on the due diligence and became known in the City as 'The two Tims'. They were a real class act and we could not have managed without them.

Roger's integration team also made significant efficiency improvements. Berger had a big factory in Bristol, which we closed, and we concentrated production at Crown's main plant at Darwen in Lancashire, which could work round the clock. We quickly got the margins up – within a couple of years, we were making half as much profit as Dulux, although their sales were about five times ours.

The twin deals really boosted our market cap. and helped our share price to recover quickly from the shock of Black Monday. In March 1988, we reached a real milestone when Williams entered the FTSE 100, only six years since Brian and I had started up. We were on a roll and, backed by our high rating, continued to buy and sell businesses at quite a speed. Our largest and most important deal in this period was about eight months after our FTSE entry, when we paid £331 million for the Pilgrim House group.

Pilgrim House had previously been called RHP, when it was Britain's largest ball-bearing manufacturer. The UK's bearings producers came under intense pressure from Japanese competition and RHP sold the business to focus on electrical and electronic engineering including Graviner, a subsidiary which made fire detection and suppression equipment, a high-growth market. Graviner had patented a unique means of detection called Fire Wire, which was used in various high-intensity environments to sense excessive heat. The aerospace industry was a major market, particularly in aero-engines, as was the defence sector where it was widely-used in tanks and other applications. Graviner also had a strong business in smoke detection.

Brian, Roger and I monitored Pilgrim House closely and made our usual first move when seriously considering a bid for a public company by acquiring a small shareholding. Then, two things happened that played into our hands. First, RHP merged with Burgess, a smaller electronic components company. The merger was not successful, there was significant tension between the two managements and the share price suffered. Pilgrim House then made a really smart move by agreeing to pay £137 million for another leading aircraft fire protection company, Kidde, which was owned by Hanson. Kidde was a mini-conglomerate, having diversified from its original core of fire protection products into areas like hot tubs and gardening equipment, which was why Hanson liked it – they could sell pieces off at a profit.

But the Kidde disposal was delayed when the US Federal Trade Commission (FTC) launched an inquiry to determine whether the prospective merger with Graviner was anti-competitive. That left Pilgrim House in limbo and we moved quickly to fill the vacuum by making an outright bid, which their board reluctantly accepted. A few months later, the FTC cleared the Kidde deal and the combination with Graviner both created a world leader in original equipment and the aftermarket, and brought us a major international presence, because Kidde was strong both in mainland Europe and the US. We knew that Hanson – since it was planning to sell the business – had run it for cash, but we were ready and able to commit the investment it needed.

We renamed the entire combined business Kidde and over the following years our money proved to have been very well spent. Moreover, as with Trevor Finn and Roger Carr, for us the acquisition uncovered a management jewel in Michael Harper, who was running Kidde. Michael proved to be a first-class chief executive. He was both an engineer and financially literate: the real deal. In fact, he would have made a great CEO of Williams – but that's a later story.

Michael had been with the engineering company Vickers for many years before joining Graviner, then part of the US conglomerate Allegheny International (which also owned Wilkinson Sword razors). Allegheny ran into deep financial trouble which forced it to sell Graviner to Pilgrim House, and they sent Michael to Minneapolis to manage Kidde just before we made our takeover bid. After the deal went through, we asked him to come back to the UK to head what became Williams' fire protection and safety division.

Supported by our financial and management resources, including Roger's special operations integration team, Michael grew the business very significantly. He knew exactly what he was doing, so I left him largely to his own devices. I told him at the outset: "Just give me a call whenever you need to – any time of the day or night. If you don't call, I'll reckon everything is OK. And if I'm not sure, I'll call you." Later, when I was chairing different companies, I would invite him to dinner from time to time with the other CEOs – it was good for them to share experiences around the table.

Kidde was a top class business, a true – and largely unsung – world leader in a growth industry. However, not all our acquisitions around this time were as successful as Pilgrim House or Crown. In fact, I have no hesitation in admitting that one of them, Smallbone Kitchens, was probably my worst ever. Not because it cost us a lot of money – it wasn't that big a deal – but because I got so many things wrong about it. Brian likes to remind me that he had absolutely nothing to do with that deal.

I started with the best of intentions: we had done very well with Rawlplug, Swish, Polycell and now Cuprinol was shaping up too, so the niche strong brand strategy that we were running in tandem with the bigger transactions had certainly proved itself. We were scouring the landscape for similar businesses and Smallbone, the up-market designer kitchen maker, seemed to fit the bill. For one thing, Lesley and I had a Smallbone kitchen and I thought the product was nice – I liked it. That was my first mistake: emotional attachment. You should never buy a company just because you like what it does. If you like it because it makes good money and has high margins – then fine. But Smallbone didn't.

A couple of guys had founded it. One had died and the other was still there. People thought it was a West Country business, but actually the two founders were from the East End of London – they decided to relocate to Devizes in Wiltshire because it created an image of 'the country' with bearded craftsmen planing away, using skills that had been passed down from generation to generation.

But that was by the by. Smallbone had gone public on the unlisted securities market (the forerunner of AIM) in the mid-eighties and then moved on to the full stock market. This was a small, friendly deal – we agreed to pay £36 million for them and they had about £3 million in net cash, which would have brought the cost down a bit. Except that, as a public company, they had to have a banking adviser. Their chairman knew someone at Goldman Sachs, which was pretty small in London then, so Smallbone hired them. The adviser was John Thornton, who had started Goldman's European M&A business and later almost became CEO of the whole bank. Goldman charged Smallbone about £2.5 million, which emptied the bank account. I was absolutely incensed and called Thornton up. He told me: "That's the game."

Legally, of course they were entirely within their rights to charge that much; the Smallbone board unanimously approved the payment and that was that. But it left a nasty taste in my mouth and for very many years after that, I would not deal with Goldman Sachs. I had to use them at Boots because they were the incumbent, but whenever I had a choice of advisers, I wouldn't retain them. I thought they had behaved disgracefully with Smallbone and my view of them hasn't changed over the years. Full of very bright people, but a culture that is over-aggressive.

Smallbone was one big mistake from start to finish. We thought that we could expand the brand down-market to capture more of the volume business. Absolutely wrong. That was one strategic mistake. Then, there was the nature of the business. Something like 40% of the sale price of the product went on getting the leads to sell it – the cost of brochures and all the other marketing activities. That is why the price of a kitchen is so high. Secondly, even though you kept producing new designs, there was no patent on designs so a skilled carpenter could reproduce a Smallbone kitchen. Obviously, he or she couldn't call it Smallbone, but that was the only restriction.

Thirdly, the cost of dealing with snagging was huge – you were sending a van out to deepest Cornwall, or somewhere. So the tail of expense on servicing was enormous. And of course, fitting the kitchen is the most sensitive part of anyone's home and if you don't get the plumbers coming in on the same day as the electricians and all the rest of it, you get very angry customers. I got a vast number of complaints from people who had been promised that their kitchen would be ready on a certain date and wasn't.

The only place we made any money was New York, where they had opened an office. There, completely unlike the UK, we got no complaints on the fitting and we made good margins. We eventually realised why – it was because the kitchens were never used, or at the very least, the owner never went into the kitchen. The maid was there, but not the owner. So, no snagging cost there either. Anyway, we got just about everything wrong and we eventually cut our losses and sold the company to its management. To be fair, it was something of an aberration because normally when we did a deal, our analysis and execution were very good. But they say you learn more from your mistakes than from your successes, and I certainly learned more than enough from that experience.

5

Pendragon

Smallbone was too small to impact Williams' performance and we were now quite a large manufacturing and building products group with a growing international presence. The one piece that didn't really fit this structure was the car dealership activities, which Trevor Finn had grown very successfully. I was responsible for managing Trevor, but he basically ran the business.

Trevor and I did one deal together which was very important, because it brought Mercedes Benz into the fold. It came about through my long-standing relationship with Keith Archbold, who had become chief executive of the vehicle subsidiary of the mini-conglomerate Blackwood Hodge (BH). In my early twenties, I had bought heavy earth-moving equipment from BH for London & Northern and in the process I had got to know Keith, who was then one of their senior finance people. He called me up one day at Williams to say that BH had decided to sell the vehicles arm and asked if we were interested in buying it.

They owned a very profitable Mercedes dealership in Leeds and were also the largest UK distributor of Fiat Iveco trucks. We were very interested in the Mercedes business and not at all in Iveco, but BH would only sell the business as a whole, so we had to take all of it. Mercedes Benz were a lot more accommodating than BMW had been, and were happy for us to take over the Leeds franchise. The problem was Iveco.

Brian and I went to a meeting at their head office in Cheshire. They were very aggressive and demanded financial guarantees and commitments for holding stock that we simply could not and would not deliver. When we refused, the Iveco managing director started a rant about how they were going to put us in our place, during which he made a big mistake: he disclosed that we represented 30–40% of their UK sales, which we had not realised and which told us that we had a valuable card in our hand.

Brian and I promptly took time out to study the balance sheet. It had very saleable freehold assets that were readily realisable, although the profitability was poor and depended on support given to dealers by Iveco. We went back into the meeting, told them we weren't prepared to be treated like serfs and I said we were going to close the business at the end of the week and they had 24 hours to remove all their stock. Not surprisingly, they were stunned – they were used to their dealers doing as they were told. But they then found us very conciliatory: we immediately agreed to open negotiations to sell the business to them. We made a small profit on this and came away from the whole BH transaction with a first class Mercedes dealership in the very prosperous city of Leeds.

Mercedes had been the vital missing link in our chain of premium car franchises. We now had a great springboard for further expansion in the industry, but at the same time car retailing was not a priority investment area for Williams. We considered a sale of the business, but in the end we settled on spinning it off into a new public company through a distribution of shares to our own investors.

Demergers like this were quite rare at the time (BAT, which was fighting a hostile bid by Sir James Goldsmith, spun off its Argos mail order and Wiggins Teape paper businesses in 1989), but we were always ready to think outside the box, and this seemed the optimum method of returning value to shareholders. We discussed the level of debt the new company should carry and the composition of its board, and then we had to decide on a name. One of our pre-listing meetings was in a conference room in a Cardiff hotel. Names were tossed around and somebody said: "This is the Pendragon room – why not Pendragon as the name?" Therefore, it became Pendragon.

Pendragon was duly listed and enjoyed largely continuous growth for almost 20 years until the financial crisis of 2008. Throughout that time, I was chairman and Trevor was CEO. We followed a pattern: we bought other dealership groups such as Evans Halshaw and Lex and we moved from being a predominantly luxury car dealer into the volume market. We also bought a small software business and developed it into a unit called Pinnacle, one of the best dealer management systems providers in the market, which Trevor later grew into a stand-alone company within Pendragon, Pinewood Technologies. Pinnacle has driven many innovations in the way that used cars in particular are bought and sold.

In order to finance Pendragon's expansion, we did a number of sale and leaseback deals on its property. These were typically set up in partnership with a bank in return for long lease and upward rent reviews, and large amounts of debt were injected into each joint venture – typically 90% debt and the rest equity, shared 50:50 between Pendragon and the funder. This worked like a charm in the benign economic conditions of the later 1990s and early 2000s.

During this period, we were doing bigger and bigger deals and with the benefit of hindsight, we became rather arrogant. We grew into the largest car dealer in Europe – the second-largest was Reg Vardy, a family-controlled business based in north-east England. The market was still highly fragmented and so in late 2005, we decided to bid for Vardy: the dealerships were a good fit regionally, their performance had largely matched ours and the family was willing to sell.

We agreed a deal but then we ran into some snags. First, one of their directors wanted to buy the business himself and started to put all sorts of obstacles in our way. Then out of the blue, Lookers, a rival retailer half our size, made a counter-bid. The situation was now getting extremely messy, so we decided to try and cut through the complexity by bidding for Lookers as well. We might well have succeeded, except that GE Capital, the finance arm of America's General Electric, had a large shareholding in Lookers.

We approached GE to see if they would sell to us, but Tony Bramall, a very smart operator who had sold his dealership business to Pendragon a couple of years earlier, then re-emerged and GE rather slyly sold its Lookers stake to him. And that was the end of our chances of taking over Lookers. That left Vardy, and we paid just over £500 million in cash for it. The banks were happy to fund a highly-leveraged Pendragon, and the market liked the deal too – our share price went up to almost 550 pence. Pendragon now had annual sales of £5 billion – quite an increase on the two-dealership business with which we had started almost 25 years earlier. When we listed Pendragon, we had about a dozen dealerships and our market cap. was about £12 million.

What happened next was one of the scariest periods of my business life. After Lehman Brothers went bust in September 2008 and triggered the financial crisis, the UK used car market collapsed. When you look back, this seems unsurprising – apart from financial services itself, the industry most exposed to the banking crisis was bound to be the car industry because, all over the world, so many cars are bought or leased through bank finance. That was certainly the case in Britain where, for a sustained period after September 2008, prices dropped by up to 10% a month. Pendragon had roughly £400 million in used car stocks, so the cash losses were enormous. You can't just sit on used car stock; it depreciates anyway, so you have to replace it – that meant our losses were being realised on a weekly basis.

The fundamental problem was one of confidence, which was a commodity in very short supply at the time. As I've said, we were heavily leveraged, and our bankers were now on full alert. We were going to breach our debt covenants within a matter of weeks – there was no question about that – and we had to come up with some sort of plan. Our lead bankers were Royal Bank of Scotland, which was quite ironic when you consider that RBS was partly responsible for causing the UK's crisis and was also the biggest single British corporate casualty of the meltdown.

You wouldn't have known that from RBS's attitude to Pendragon. After they had been bailed out by the British government, we were placed in their high risk/recovery division. I had heard about the behaviour of bankers during this period, but I had never come across a more unpleasant and arrogant group of people in my life. Bizarrely, given what had happened to their company, they seemed drunk on the power they had over their clients. They weren't making any money, yet they came into the meeting and behaved like gangsters. They were horrible.

During one meeting, we came up with a plan to staunch the losses and get back to at least break-even, including selling down large chunks of property and so on. Looking across the table, I said that we could manage our way out if we were given time. One of the RBS people said in a hugely arrogant way: "You don't control the business – we do."

I was so incensed that I took my car keys out of my pocket and threw them at him along with an expletive. Then I said: "Well, you run the business and don't forget that we are the biggest car dealer in Britain and if we go under, the value of every dealer in the country will collapse." Then I walked out.

I immediately rang Stephen Hester, the former chief executive of British Land who had been put in as CEO of RBS after the bank's collapse and virtual nationalisation. We had got to know each other over the years, principally meeting in the shooting field. In my dealings with Stephen, I have always found him very straightforward. I asked him to call off the dogs.

In the meantime, Trevor and I had started a conversation with the Department for Business. Lord (Mervyn) Davies had taken a surprise peerage to join the Labour government. I had known Mervyn in his days as CEO of Standard Chartered bank and I had played golf with him in Hong Kong with a mutual friend. I rang him to set up a meeting. Trevor and I wrote a paper, which proposed that the government incentivise consumers to scrap older cars by making money available to part-fund the purchase of a new car. This would put a floor under the market. A similar scrappage scheme had been set up by the Italian government and had been very effective.

We couldn't prove it, but we believed that the crisis was all about confidence and that the net cost of the scheme would not be great. It would stimulate new car purchases and the resulting VAT receipts would more than compensate for the amount the government would pay to buyers. A lot of these really old cars were owned by older people, and due to the leasing arrangements possible at that time, you could put them in new cars using the government-funded deposit.

Mervyn listened carefully and agreed to speak to Peter (now Lord) Mandelson, his Secretary of State. Peter got it and said he would press the Treasury for action. The Treasury always says no and abhors interventionism, but this was an extraordinary situation and Peter put all of his considerable influence behind the taking of action. Within a couple of weeks, we had a scheme, and within weeks of that being implemented, the price of second hand cars stabilised and even started to rise. And it reduced the age of the UK car parc substantially. Peter Mandelson has a mixed reputation, but in this and other matters where I have been involved, he was by a long way one of the best business ministers I ever dealt with.

I also managed to get a meeting with Stephen Hester and told him in some detail about my experience with his recovery team. I never threatened, but he was left in no doubt that, if they didn't start to behave reasonably, I would do everything in my power to expose their bad behaviour. I told him that I would not abandon Pendragon and I would see that RBS got its money back. Stephen made sure the message got down to the RBS team. The personnel were changed and within days, we had a deal. It was expensive and involved a deeply-discounted rights issue. The banks all took options and within months made a handsome profit. Within three years, the debt was reduced dramatically.

I could have stepped down as chairman of Pendragon some time before the crisis – I had been there for 26 years, almost 20 of them when it was a public company. But I could see something bad coming – obviously, no-one knew how bad – and I made the decision to stay and help deal with whatever problems there were. I have no doubt that was the right decision. And there is no question that my clout with RBS and relationship with Mervyn prevented a disaster. I put all my weight and reputation behind the effort to save the company from going bust, and there is no question that the scrappage scheme saved the whole industry. It was a simple thing – a very simple thing. But it required a sea change in the government's mindset.

After all the trauma, I thought that I should move on, safe in the knowledge that Pendragon had been rescued and was viable again. I told Trevor: "I'm just getting a bit too old for this." Trevor was tremendous fun to be with, a really talented guy. We'd worked together since 1982 and it was now 2010.

He continued to run the business until 2019, when he retired – that must make him one of the longest-serving CEOs in modern company history.

Even before the shocking impact of Covid-19, Pendragon (along with the rest of the car industry) began to have a hard time because of the government's anti-diesel policy. This has done enormous damage to the manufacturers as well as the dealers. Yes, there is a problem with diesel emissions, but the modern diesel cars are much cleaner and the industry should have been given more time to adapt. It would have been much better to launch a scrappage scheme on old diesel cars and trucks, because they are the problem.

We didn't get everything right at Pendragon. When we were laying down the growth strategy, we thought that by being really big we would have more buying power with the manufacturers. But actually, that didn't really work: the bigger you got, the more aggressive they became with you and the more frightened they were of you. You became a threat to them. And the new car business is all based on incentives for volume and the OEMs play real games with you.

It is, fundamentally, a master–serf relationship. With Mercedes Benz or BMW, if there was a very popular model and you behaved yourself and did all the right things, then they allocated more of that model to you. The converse was that they could make you sell less attractive cars. The fact of the matter is that, if you owned eight BMW dealerships and did everything they told you, you (personally) did very well. These businesses made a million a year or whatever, you invested some of it back into the business and you had a very, very comfortable life. If you looked at the *Sunday Times* Rich List 10 or 15 years ago, probably every tenth person on it was a car dealer.

And it was a peculiar relationship. The area managers working for the manufacturers had the power to materially increase or reduce your profit: a master–serf relationship with a difference. If you played it right, your business could become a very rich serf, and Trevor handled the relationship very well.

However, like all very long-serving CEOs, I think Trevor eventually became quite resistant to the idea of handing over to a successor. I foresaw that this might be the case, so when I left Pendragon I arranged for a strong chairman to take over from me. Mike Davies, a former colleague from Williams, fitted the bill. The problems arose after Mike retired.

I was still a shareholder and I expressed my view that Trevor should retire to the non-executive directors. The executive team needed a thorough overhaul. There were good people, such as Martin Casha the chief operating officer, still there, but many of the others were mediocre. By the time Chris Chambers became chairman, it was really too late. The market was changing beyond recognition, largely due to the government's onslaught on diesel cars. In desperation, Pendragon embarked on a strategy to focus on the second-hand market, but this hugely increased stocks just when prices were collapsing. Trevor left in 2019.

It's a salutary lesson. Trevor was brilliant for many years, but in the end he stayed too long and I think he came to believe that Pendragon was his company. He therefore failed to move with the times – which were very difficult – and he paid the price. That said, his achievement should never be forgotten: he built a great company, one of the largest car dealerships in the world, and both he and I had enormous fun in the process.

6

Racal and Tyco

The 1980s were a fantastic decade for Williams – when the 10-year reviews came out in the papers at the end of 1989, we were one of the top stock market performers. However, we were aware that things were changing as we went into the 1990s and we were determined not to stand still.

First, we sold Crown Berger, the UK and Ireland paints business, to Nobel of Sweden, which later merged with Akzo in the Netherlands to create AkzoNobel. It was less than four years since we had created that business through the acquisitions from Reed and Hoechst, but the day that Williams bought a company, we always had an idea of whom we would sell to, if and when we wanted to divest.

By the same token, we thought strategically in identifying acquisitions – hence we often took small stakes in potential targets long before we made a bid for them. We had bought a stake in Yale & Valor, the locks business, in 1988, held it for three years and then in 1991 we reached an agreement to buy the company for about £330 million.

The acquisition process itself was tortuous with the final stages bordering on farce. Michael Montague was Yale's chairman and he was quite idiosyncratic. I got on with him pretty well but he was always saying to me: "I'd like to do a deal with you, but Brian doesn't like me." This wasn't true but it was a neat way for Michael to play hard to get.

One afternoon, we finally reached what we thought was an agreement, so we lined up BZW and Schroders to organise the financing: we planned to raise between £100m and £200m through a stock market placing. This was all set up to be done at 7.00 am the following morning, when we would be announcing the deal.

Brian and I were staying at a flat in London and had to be at Schroders in Cheapside at 6.45 am. I am quite keen on breakfast, particularly when the day is likely to be a long one, but we didn't have time to eat at the flat so Brian said we could get everything we would want at Schroders – bacon sandwiches, croissants, the lot. We had just arrived at Cheapside when we got a call from Yale saying that they weren't happy with the deal that had been negotiated. They were going to have a board meeting later in the day to discuss it. There was no point sitting around at Schroders, so we left – still without having had any breakfast. We went back to our London office and spent most of the rest of the morning in phone calls which ran on through lunchtime. So no time for food then, either.

Eventually, we were told that the Yale board meeting was at a hotel near Earl's Court and we arranged to meet Michael Montague there at 7.00 pm. Brian and I went by ourselves to the hotel, which was pretty crummy, intending to nail down the deal. We were told that Michael was in a private room, so we went in and found the whole board there, tucking into their dinner. Big, juicy steaks and the works.

Michael asked us: "Have you eaten?" and we said we hadn't. Then he said: "We'll get you something later. Here's the key to my room. I'll come up shortly and we can talk." So – feeling even more famished after seeing what the Yale board were devouring – we went upstairs and walked down a dingy corridor to find Michael's room. Brian remarked: "I bet Lord Hanson doesn't have to do this sort of thing."

We got into the room and about half an hour later, Michael appeared with his finance director. The room was cramped, so someone sat on the bed and someone else sat on the chest of drawers and we set about trying to finalise this £400m deal.

After that, things got really weird. Michael asked if we had had dinner yet and I said, very firmly: "No!" So he called room service and asked: "What can you do straight away?" And the receptionist obviously answered: "What would you like?" At which point, for some reason – maybe because it had been a long day for him, too – Michael launched into a tirade, shouting at the receptionist and demanding to talk to the manager. Then he slammed down the phone. After about 20 minutes, there was a knock at the door, Michael opened it and there was the manageress who told him: "You have been very rude to one of my staff and reduced her to tears. I want you to leave the hotel." Michael said: "I'm not leaving," and slammed the door in her face. So that was our last chance of getting any food gone.

Half an hour later, we had basically settled on terms and needed to let our respective boards and teams of advisers know, so Michael picked up the phone and the operator said: "I'm sorry, I've been told to cut off your line and not accept any calls from this room." Michael turned to us and said: "We'll use the FD's room. They won't have cut him off." I spoke to our board from there – no mobile phones in those days – and Brian went out into the street, found a phone box and called Schroders and BZW. We got back to the flat at about 1.00 am and made ourselves a sandwich.

After the Yale & Valor saga, we identified a bid target which, had we succeeded in buying it, would have been a fantastic acquisition for Williams. This was Racal Electronics, which was a classic case of a poorly performing business whose assets were, as a result, very undervalued.

In the 1980s Racal had created Vodafone, which was then called Racal Telecom, and I personally did a lot of work on Racal while it still owned Vodafone. They had spun off 20% of it in the late eighties to defeat a hostile takeover bid and then promised to demerge the other 80% by September 1991. It was quite clear to me that, if you took out the value of Vodafone, the stock market was attributing a negative value to the rest of Racal, despite the fact that it owned Chubb security and one of Britain's largest defence electronics businesses.

I realised that people didn't like and didn't value this company. And it was clear that the Vodafone demerger was not going to change this quickly. So, straight after the demerger, when for the first time Racal Electronics was being valued on its own – and not very highly – I rang its chairman, Sir Ernest Harrison, who was a Racal legend (having been with the company for more than 40 years), and told him that we'd like to buy the company. He refused to see or talk to me and then he went to Corfu on holiday.

With John Major

Racal was a perfect Williams target. It had about £650 million of assets and was making profit margins of just 1% on annual sales of £1.6 billion. Chubb was a very strong brand. The defence business was a leader in the military radio market. So we decided to launch an all-shares hostile bid which valued Racal at about £750 million. We caught Ernie on the hop but, as we expected, he fought back hard including a commitment to de-merge Chubb.

Brian and I went round the Racal shareholders and got a lot of traction, although it was clear from the outset that Ernie had considerable residual backing from big investors who had been with Racal a long time. For example, Carol Galley at Mercury Asset Management – who was one of the most influential fund managers at the time – was supportive of Ernie. In fairness to him, he had made them a lot of money over the years, especially from Vodafone, and so there was a loyalty factor which we knew we had to overcome.

What didn't help us was the fact we couldn't use our usual City advisers, because both Schroders and BZW were conflicted. Schroders had done some work for Racal and BZW had been working for Tomkins, which was thinking about trying to buy Chubb. So our trusted advisers were not by our side – and that was a big mistake. Instead, we used Justin Dowley and Guy Dawson at Morgan Grenfell, who were very good but obviously we didn't know each other as well as we knew our long-standing advisers. That can make a vital difference in hostile battles, where the decision-making margins are very fine. It was a lesson to me that you don't go into battle without all of your generals.

The crucial moment came when we had to raise our bid. Unlike our two previous hostile bid targets, McKechnie and Norcros, Racal warranted a higher offer: apart from its hugely undervalued assets, it was dripping with overheads which Roger would have cut immediately. The value of our first offer had declined to about 50p a share since we made it because our share price had fallen, so the situation was different from the virtuous circle that we had created in our bid for J. & H. B. Jackson, when our share price had risen during the contest and therefore increased the value of our offer.

It was hard to determine what was causing the share price to fall. Possibly there was concern in the market that we weren't going to win. Or some people thought we might be over-reaching ourselves in buying Racal. In any event, our advisers accurately fed back to us that shareholders wanted some cash as well as Williams paper. The big question was how much we should increase the bid by.

Our advisers thought that if we tweaked the price then we would probably get over the line. Brian and I had a long discussion, and for one of the very few times in our partnership, we disagreed about the best course of action. Brian's view was that if we increased the bid by too much, this would be counter-productive and reinforce the view that Racal was a step too far for Williams, thereby triggering a further fall in our share price and undermining the value of our increased terms. He thought, like the advisers, that we could win with a small increase in price and that, having won, our share price would then jump.

I had a different view – I thought that we had to win the thing first, and to win it we needed to make a bigger increase in the offer. We had a long-standing agreement that we would never do anything if one of us didn't want to do it, so we increased the bid but not by much: we added 10p of cash to the original offer, which meant our final bid was worth about 55p a share. And it wasn't enough. A number of key institutions supported Racal and we fell short by about 7%. If we'd increased the bid to 60p a share, we would almost certainly have won – that would have been enough to overcome the loyalty that many investors felt they owed Ernie.

Losing was a huge disappointment because it would undoubtedly have been one of the great deals. I was really cross at the time, but I had a lot of admiration for Ernie Harrison. He just didn't want his great Racal record to end like that, and he fought very hard to make sure it didn't.

As big moments like this invariably prove in business, it was a watershed for Williams. For some years there had been three of us at the top of the company – Brian, Roger and me – rather than the original two. Roger was really running the businesses, I was doing the M&A ideas and strategy stuff, and after the dust settled on the Racal bid, Brian simply felt that he had done what he wanted to do and it was time to leave. So very amicably, he stepped down as CEO and literally went fishing, which was one of his passions. He was eventually lured back into business by House of Fraser, to lead its stock market IPO.

He and I were very different in what we personally wanted from being in business: Brian, in his own words, did it because it paid well and financed his leisure time. I was certainly not a workaholic, but for me business has always been a vocation.

We had had an unforgettable 12 years together and, along with all the hard work, it had been a lot of fun, which should be part of the point. Building something from scratch, as we had done with Williams, is very special and not many people get to do it. But change is the essence of business and the successful executive is the one who recognises rather than resists that. Brian knew that, for him, it was time to move on.

Roger became CEO and the two of us set about re-orientating Williams. Strategically, I recognised that the world was turning against public companies that were seen as conglomerates. Hanson had failed with an attempt to take over ICI about the same time that we bid for Racal, and BTR was starting to run out of steam. 'Focus' was becoming the new buzzword, and we decided to concentrate on three areas of business – fire, security and branded home products - and pull out of the other two that we still had.

We sold our engineering division to a management buy-out and enhanced the home products portfolio by buying Hammerite from the mini-conglomerate Hunting. Hammerite was an amazing little deal: it was based in Prudhoe in Northumberland and its metal paint was one that I had known as a boy with my bike – it encapsulated iron or other metals to stop the oxidising process of rust, so it was used on railings, garden furniture, bikes, anything vulnerable to rust. Really, it was a toxic mix of black gunk. We paid about £8 million for it and it was making about £1 million a year.

We quickly realised that the price was completely elastic (excuse the irresistible pun) because when someone went to buy a can of Hammerite there was no other product like it on the market. So you went into your B&Q store or Halfords or wherever and bought it virtually regardless of the cost. You wouldn't know whether it was £2.40 or £3.80 because you just wanted Hammerite. So we kept putting up the price.

The retailers quite liked this, because their sales didn't go down – in fact, sales went up and the stores were making more of a margin all the time. Then we started to export it, we did all sorts of things to expand the market, and by the time we sold the business five years later, it was making about £13 million profit on sales of £25 million. We sold it to ICI as a part of a package of branded home products, so it's hard to gauge what it went for, but effectively they paid about £150 million for it. In terms of increasing shareholder value, Hammerite was one of the best things we ever did.

Shortly after buying Hammerite, we made another smart move when we appointed a new public relations company. I had first met Roland Rudd when he was a journalist at the Financial Times. One day in 1994, he called me and asked me to lunch at Brooks's Club in St. James's Street. He confided that he was going to start a financial PR firm and he wanted Williams to be a client. He came up with a great pitch – Williams had the worst PR in the FTSE 100, Roland assured me. So we should give him a chance to improve our image.

I wasn't completely sure, but I have always admired individuals who have the guts to start a business. So I struck a deal – we would pay Finsbury, Roland's new firm, £10,000 in advance for doing a project for us, and if it worked out we would appoint him as our adviser. I wanted him to have some cash flow to pay his first month's salaries. The project went well, we duly appointed them and Roland went on to act for me for many years, not only at Williams but also at other major companies that I went on to chair, including Pilkington, Boots and Heathrow. I made one mistake: I should have asked for a share in the business because Roland became hugely successful – and deservedly so.

Finsbury had plenty to do for Williams, because five years after we failed to win Racal, we went back for Chubb. By now of course it had been demerged, and we ended up paying a very full price for it – almost £1.3 billion. When you remember that we could have got it along with the rest of Racal for about £800 million, you can see what a great deal Racal would have been, both in terms of price and timing. I suppose that also proves our analysis of Racal being hugely undervalued was spot on, but that's not much consolation.

Our reason for buying Chubb was very logical. It was a tremendous fit with Yale & Valor and gave us a really strong position in both the home and commercial security markets, and in both physical and electronic security. It also made our security division a very attractive commodity to a future buyer. But the stock market gave us no credit for any of this. The deal was not well received in the City, where we were seen to have overpaid.

In a way, that was the beginning of the end of Williams, because the market reaction told me that we were never again going to get a premium price for our shares. We had dropped out of the FTSE 100 and were still viewed as a conglomerate, despite our concentration on fewer businesses which we had built into market leaders. And that set me thinking about what we should do strategically. One of the most important things in business, but also one of the hardest for the people involved to accept, is realising when the game is over and that shareholders deserve better than just to have a company which is treading water, not really going anywhere.

I still felt there was a lot of value in Williams. It was just that, under the present structure and management, we had reached a crossroads. The first move we made was to sell the branded home products business – Polycell, Polyfilla, Hammerite, Cuprinol etc – to ICI for a very good price of £350 million. That meant we were now a focused industrial business like many other major companies, with two divisions – security and fire protection – holding strong market positions.

That, combined with our relatively low rating, made us attractive to predators – and after the ICI disposal, one quickly appeared. This was the big American conglomerate Tyco, which had grown rapidly through a series of acquisitions including in security and fire protection, and was now much larger than us. In fact, Tyco had tried to buy Kidde before the Williams deal and Pilgrim House fended them off. They had also tried to tempt Michael Harper to join them by offering him a £2m package – Michael turned it down. Tyco was driven by its CEO Dennis Kozlowski and his finance director Mark Swartz, who first approached us in late 1998. We rebuffed them, but the following year they flew over in the company Gulfstream to propose an all-share takeover of Williams.

From the start, I was suspicious of them – their acquisition-led expansion had been fuelled by very highly-rated paper – but I was even more disturbed when they started to explain how they wanted to conduct the deal. They intended to agree the transaction and then take several months to complete it, during which time Williams would write down assets and lower its profitability, presumably so that they could write them back up at a later date, after the acquisition.

I was fundamentally against this, not just because I was chairman but because I was the only major shareholder on the board. An all-share deal would leave every investor with Tyco stock, and I wondered how sustainable the value of the shares was. We flew to New York to give them our response, and I decided to stay at arm's length while Roger led the Williams team in meetings and reported back to me on the detail of Tyco's offer. As chairman, I felt that I should hold back, keep my distance and not get sucked into meetings. Kozlowski and Swartz reiterated their all-share terms and also offered Roger and me an incentive – they proposed to give me a huge pay-off and to retain Roger, who would be on a fantastic remuneration package.

Roger wanted to do the deal, but the more I looked at the bid terms, the less I liked them. So I refused to put the Tyco offer to the board unless it was a cash offer. I knew that this would kill the deal and so it did. Tyco walked away and there was a lot of disappointment in the market. But when I took our non-executive directors – who included Sir Michael Bishop, founder of the airline British Midland and later Lord Glendonbrook, and Sir Victor Blank, later chairman of Lloyds Bank – through what had happened, they were horrified that we had even considered doing a deal with Tyco.

Our judgment proved correct. Tyco's share price eventually blew up and on top of that, Kozlowski and Swartz were later convicted in a US court on various counts of falsifying business records and securities fraud. Had we accepted their paper, Williams investors would have suffered heavy losses.

However, we still had to confront the fact that had rendered Williams vulnerable in the first place – we were stuck in a rut. We had good businesses, but our ability to move the earnings as fast as the City wished was becoming a problem. The share price had underperformed since Roger had replaced Brian as CEO, and continued to value the business at significantly below the sum of its parts; our ability to use our paper to make acquisitions was non-existent; and the growing private equity presence in the market and the PE firms' ability to use debt to enhance returns put us at a continuing and distinct disadvantage.

Roger and I discussed this, and his instinct was to continue to cut costs in order to meet analysts' earnings expectations. However, we had also acquired some very low-quality manned guarding businesses to augment Chubb's presence in this segment of the security market, and the drawback of this strategy was that it diluted the quality of our earnings. The problem came home to roost a few years later after we demerged into Chubb and Kidde.

There is no doubt that, as executive chairman, I had not concentrated enough on what we could do to break out of this trap. With hindsight, it was a classic case of my having been there too long. However, the matter was about to be taken out of my hands, at least for the time being.

I received a call one day from Sir David Rowe-Ham, a former stockbroker and Lord Mayor of London, who was one of our three non-executive directors along with Sir Michael and Sir Victor. David asked me to meet with them, and at the meeting they told me that there was widespread dissatisfaction in the investment community with the company's performance, and that shareholders wanted changes in the senior management. They were quite blunt in saying that I had taken my eye off the ball, and that while Roger had many abilities, Williams now needed a CEO who would drive top-line growth and that was not Roger's forte.

They asked me to consider the situation over the next week or two, but made it clear that the solution would have to involve changes at the top. It was tough to hear that message – since Brian's departure, Roger and I had led the group in close partnership for many years. But the truth always hurts, as the saying goes, and they were right. Williams had completely lost its way.

So I came to terms with the situation and we met again after a few days and decided on a plan. I would step down from my executive position and become non-executive chairman. Meanwhile, Michael Harper would be asked to replace Roger as CEO.

This was all agreed and I prepared to break the news to Roger the following Monday. But on the Sunday, I got a call at home from David Rowe-Ham. He told me that he had had second thoughts about the situation – even though he had started the whole process – and that, while he thought I should retire as a sop to the City, the disruption caused by Roger also leaving the business would be too great. I will never know if he was making a play to be chairman. Strange behaviour. I immediately rang Michael and Victor, and they were flabbergasted. David, who died in 2020, spoke to me years later, apologised and confessed that he had panicked.

You should learn lessons from any bad experience, and the lesson I took to heart from this was that, when a decision of this magnitude is agreed, all those concerned have to commit to it in writing. I subsequently did exactly that with the non-executives at Invensys in the case of our CEO there, Ulf Henriksson.

I told Michael and Victor that we should not make these very significant changes without unanimity among the NEDs – and in any case, the board maths made it impossible. So, while we all returned for the short term to business as usual, the wake-up call had hit home and I knew we had to find an alternative solution which also involved fundamental change. Over the next few months, we evolved the strategy to demerge Williams into two separate entities, Chubb and Kidde, and to sell the low-margin former Yale locks business. It was the exception in the Security division which was largely focused on higher-value services rather than lock manufacturing, and was bought by Assa Abloy of Sweden.

We then had to decide who was going to do what. Chubb was the larger business, but I didn't want anything to do with it. Even with locks gone, its quality of earnings had become poor and I did not rank the CEO highly. But Roger rated him and was happy to become chairman of Chubb. I opted to take the non-executive chairmanship at Kidde with Michael Harper as CEO. We appointed a really good board, including one of my longest-standing business contacts, Michael Kirkwood, the former head of Citigroup in the UK. Michael became a close friend as well as a colleague and we have shared many golf rounds and shoots over the years. As Michael says, it's almost an attraction of opposites: he is a public schoolboy and graduate from Scotland and I'm a grammar school boy from the Midlands who never went to university.

We get along famously, although I think he found my style of chairmanship a bit different from the norm. I like to think that I'm a good conductor of the board orchestra – I've been the lead violinist, so I know how the strings are feeling and when to bring them in. My view is that the boardroom should be somewhere for the directors to reach and formalise consensual agreement – not an arena for hours of argument. If anyone has a particular issue, I want to deal with that literally outside the room, away from the actual board meeting. This approach facilitates decision-making and prevents any kind of grandstanding, which I hate. Michael said he had encountered very few chairs who were as keen on getting on with board business and ensuring that our meetings didn't take too long.

Although Kidde was just over half the size of Chubb by annual sales, I had no doubt that it was by far the better-quality company. This was despite the fact that we left it with the Chubb fire and smoke detection and alarm business, which would have fitted better with Kidde. There was a continuing relationship between the two businesses, because Kidde was one of Chubb's preferred suppliers.

The demerger took effect in July 2000. I immediately sold all my shares in Chubb, which turned out to be a smart move: Chubb subsequently ran into various problems and struggled. It was demerged at 255p a share and within three years was taken over by America's United Technologies Corporation (UTC) for 75p. Roger left a few months before the takeover bid and was succeeded by Sir Bob Horton, the former CEO of BP.

Because of Chubb's position as a major customer, we took a close interest in the UTC takeover. Michael Harper got to know UTC well and one day, about two years after the Chubb takeover and after I had retired from the board, the UTC guy who ran Chubb came to see him. He told Michael that they realised they had bought the wrong company – they should have bought Kidde and now they wanted to do precisely that. They eventually offered 165p a share, which valued Kidde at £1.44 billion. That was a pretty good increase from the 69.5p a share at which it had started life on demerger. And, with a final flourish, it brought the curtain down on the Williams era.

It's very important in business to distinguish between fads, which are temporary, and structural change, which is permanent. The market is prone to embrace fashions – the late 1990s dot.com boom being a classic case. As a business leader, it's possible – and usually advisable – to look through these phases because it's highly likely that the fashion will change and fundamentals will reassert themselves.

Of course, you have to move with the times. Dot.com mania reflected a technological revolution which gave birth to new companies such as Amazon, but it also embraced many other firms, which disappeared in a puff of smoke when the boom bust. And, during that period, the market ignored the opportunities for established firms to move with the times and adopt the new technology themselves. The British retailer Next, which has been so successful online, is a good example of such evolution. But as I write this, we are witnessing what I see as another bubble. Time will tell, for example, whether companies like Cazoo will really disrupt the used car business. I have huge doubts about its business model and even bigger doubts about its current valuation. We shall see.

By contrast with the dot.com craze, the demise of the conglomerates was due to a permanent change in the business landscape. This has impacted most of the diversified Western groups that flourished in the late twentieth century, including America's General Electric (GE), the most celebrated of them all.

Williams was a creature of that time and prospered in the halcyon days of the conglomerates. But as the 1990s developed, we recognised that the world was changing and I think we adapted better than most of our peers. Like us, Hanson broke itself up. But BTR got completely stuck and merged with Siebe to create Invensys, which was a disaster – as I later found out at first hand.

All of us – Hanson, BTR, Williams and the rest – ultimately owed our success in the 1980s to our superior share rating. That's what enabled us to make earnings-enhancing acquisitions, and it was based on persuading the market that we should enjoy a premium for management. Shareholders had to believe that, because of the management factor, the value of our companies was greater than the sum of their parts. During the 1990s, the market became increasingly less willing to attach a premium to conglomerate management, which is why our ratings started to slip.

There were several reasons for this. For one thing, analysts got smarter and started to value organic growth higher than acquisition growth. But the biggest single reason was the mutation of the venture capital industry – which had originally focused on fostering start-up and early stage businesses – into private equity (PE), which specialised in buying all or parts of public companies. Because they were off-market and enjoyed favourable tax status, the PE firms could pay higher prices than the publicly-quoted conglomerates, inject more leverage and get higher equity returns – thereby attracting more institutional investment, enabling them to raise bigger funds and buy more businesses. It's a giant snowball, which is still rolling. The publicly-listed conglomerates could not compete with PE. They had to evolve or die, and Williams recognised that imperative with our demerger.

7

East Midlands Electricity

I took my first non-executive Directorship in 1990. I hadn't deliberately planned to start a NED career – Williams was going strong
and taking a lot of my time – but I was approached by Spencer
Stuart, one of the leading London head-hunter firms, to see whether
I would join the board of East Midlands Electricity (EME).

EME was one of the 12 Regional Electricity Companies (RECs)
in England and Wales responsible for power distribution and supply.
They were the old area electricity boards and were being floated
on the stock market as part of the government's privatisation of
the electricity industry. The head-hunters were therefore having a
field day finding NEDs to join the new boards that the companies
needed before they went public.

Being an East Midlander, I of course had a strong local connection. And EME's head office was in Nottingham, which was very
convenient for me. So I agreed to go on the board, and I spent a
lot of time in the ensuing couple of months working through the
prospectus and pre-flotation plans. The electricity generators were
also being privatised, so the whole thing was a major exercise. The
government rented a huge building somewhere and all the different
company boards were in there, going through all this material.

The dominant figure on the board was John Harris, an electrical
engineer by training, who was both chairman and chief executive. Of course, you wouldn't have that combination of roles today

because corporate governance wouldn't allow it, but it was still fairly common in 1990. The rest of the board comprised a couple of executives – finance director and operations director – and a number of local worthies, the most senior of whom was Nicholas Corah, a very nice man who ran an old-established textile business in Leicester which was a big clothing supplier to Marks & Spencer.

Although its job was to supply electricity, EME was really three or four different businesses: the 'wires' operation, which distributed power from the National Grid to homes and businesses, the supply business, small-scale electricity generation activity and a very, very strange organisation which was called retail. Retail – as those old enough to remember will know – was a chain of showroom shops, which sold electrical appliances and, most importantly, collected cash from customers because it was the place people went to pay their electricity bills. All of the RECs had these retail arms.

So the privatisation went ahead and at the first few board meetings, it was very apparent that John Harris realised the business was hugely overstaffed and inefficient. His basic philosophy was to take some cost out of the business, generate cash and invest it in other non-regulated businesses – in other words, to become a conglomerate. At the time, of course, conglomerates were still viewed positively, so I thought that this was generally a reasonable strategy.

First, though, I concentrated on getting accurate financial information particularly about the showroom business, where I asked for detailed accounts. I had great difficulty in extracting these from the business and, when I finally received them, I soon realised why: it was very apparent that these shops were hugely loss-making. However, they were shown to be profitable in the published accounts because a per capita sum was transferred from the supply business to the retail business for collecting the money from consumers. This sum was out of all proportion to how much it actually cost to do this, so the profitability was completely artificial.

Another rather bizarre thing about EME was that it was spending quite a lot of money on advertising electricity – they even had the Nottingham Forest manager Brian Clough on their adverts. This surprised me, to put it mildly, since the only place you could buy electricity in the East Midlands was from East Midlands Electricity. The market was later opened up by the industry regulator, then called Offer, but that hadn't happened yet. I thought that the whole thing was a very strange set-up.

John Harris then started taking out cash costs. But he did the cost reduction in a calculated way, with an eye on the next regulatory review of pricing. Under the privatised system, Offer would rule every five years on how much the RECs could raise their prices, and based its ruling on the companies' profitability. John Harris believed that he should not show too much cost reduction to the regulator too early on, because by keeping some back he would both get a better regulatory settlement and have a cushion of further costs that he could take out to keep profits moving up over the next five years. It was a big flaw in the system: the regulatory set-up mitigated against taking out all the costs that a company could cut, which would maximise the efficiency of the business – and limit price increases for consumers.

Harris also set about buying businesses in a dash to become a conglomerate. He wanted to build a significant maintenance business in the region, so his first acquisitions were electrical contractors – firms that employed electricians to fix electricity faults in council houses, small estates and so on. They tended to be small businesses with very few financial controls, and the amount of due diligence that EME carried out was clearly negligible. And of course, as we shall see shortly, those acquisitions went horribly wrong.

John Harris also spent a lot of time in the policy unit at 10 Downing Street. He was always off to talk to politicians, and it became apparent at one board meeting that he was doing this because the government was trying to persuade him to buy what was left of the British coal industry.

After the miners' strike ended in 1985, British Coal had really cut back the size of the industry and now the government wanted to privatise what was left. There was a small open cast coal company called Budge Mining, which wanted to take over British Coal, so the politicians proposed a joint venture between EME and Budge, in which Budge would run the operations while we provided the cash to fund them from our cash flow. When I finally got to the bottom of the proposed deal, it was terrible. We were going to get a percentage of the notional profits while taking all the risk – both financial and reputational. And environmental – the issues around closing mines had not been factored in at all.

While these talks were going on, the non-core acquisitions that EME had made started to lose money. Nicholas Corah, who was effectively deputy chairman – senior independent director in today's terms – and I persuaded John Harris to appoint a chief operating officer. We advertised the job and hired Norman Askew, who had been at the engineering company TI Group. He very quickly realised how badly-run the business was and the losses that were being accumulated.

I was just a NED – I don't think I was even chairman of audit or remuneration. But looking round the boardroom, it dawned on me that when the full extent of the disaster was seen by the outside world, then I would take the blame – because I was the one person who had a City reputation and should have known better than to let this happen.

I realised that we had to change the chief executive, and I called Nicholas Corah. He agreed with me, but said that it would be messy because John Harris was held in high regard in Downing Street, and so on. But I insisted and I said that, if we didn't make the change, I was going to resign. He got quite frightened at that, but I said that while I wouldn't make a big thing about leaving and would just disappear quietly, I was no longer prepared to stand for what we were doing.

Nicholas then went to talk to the other NEDs, who were people from small businesses in and around the East Midlands. And to his amazement, they all said: "Why has it taken so long for you guys to think what we have been thinking?" Then Nicholas and I went to see Norman Askew and asked him if he would take over as CEO. He agreed, but while John Harris was still there, he couldn't make any move or give any indication that this is what he would do. It was up to us.

I had no ambition to be chairman, so I suggested that Nicholas take the chair while Norman became chief executive. At that point, the other NEDs came to see me and said: "Look, Nigel – Nicholas is a very nice guy but we need somebody quite strong in here and you are the only person on the board who could do the job." Norman had also told me that he didn't think Nicholas would be an appropriate chairman, and pressed me to take the post on.

I agreed and went along to see John Harris and tell him that the board had unanimously decided that he had to go. It came completely out of the blue to him and he was furious. He started shouting at me, telling me that I knew nothing about the electricity industry, I was just an accountant and that I would regret it. I simply said: "Well that's the way it is, John. You can either like it or not." He stormed out of the office and I never saw him again.

I became chairman on 1 May 1994 and Norman became CEO and we immediately grasped the nettle of the retail business, which John Harris had not dealt with. Other RECs had realised, as we had, that their retail businesses were loss-makers, so what several of us did was bundle them all into one company called Powerhouse and sell them off. A few years later, they were bought by a New Zealand venture capital entity, but they were competing with the big specialist retailers and without the cross-subsidy from collecting customers' electricity bill payments, they were bereft. Eventually, Powerhouse went bust.

Norman and I then sat down and decided on a strategy. The retail business had gone and we started closing all the other little bits of businesses that had been bought at quite large cost. We downsized from the huge head office just north of Nottingham to a smaller office nearby, which cut costs further.

Among our peripheral interests was a half-share in a combined cycle gas-fired power station in Corby, Northamptonshire, where we had invested with Hawker Siddeley, the electrical engineering manufacturer. Hawker Siddeley was taken over by BTR in what proved to be BTR's last big hostile takeover. BTR didn't want to keep Corby either and I had to deal with its Australian chief executive, Alan Jackson. That was a bit weird, because he was into all sorts of schemes about how to deconsolidate the business. It was all about accounting and nothing to do with the business at all.

But Corby was a minor matter compared with the really big question we faced, which concerned the future of the core electricity business. It became very, very clear soon after privatisation that having 12 regional companies was a nonsense, and there was an awful lot of talk about merging. The mergers that made most obvious sense were with contiguous companies, so we talked to Midlands Electricity and Eastern Electricity. The terrible thing was that all these discussions fell down because, in these other companies, the old electricity board chairmen or chief executives were still there and it was all about them – they wanted to be executive chairman and/or CEO of the merged group. We thought that was inappropriate, and so these deals never came to anything. A classic case of the 'social issues' blocking something that made total business sense.

Norman and I thought we were back to square one. But then, something peculiar happened: East Midlands – and a number of the other RECs – became attractive to foreign buyers, particularly Americans. Our investment bank advisers took a call from a bank acting for Dominion Resources, which was based in Richmond, Virginia and owned Virginia Power, the state generating and supply company. They wanted to buy East Midlands, and were prepared to put quite a high price on it.

Norman, I and the board discussed this and we felt that, at the price they were intimating, it was a deal we could not turn down on behalf of the shareholders. The price was attractive and particularly so because we thought the regulatory environment would get tougher, thus profits would drop every five years and we'd end up returning a figure which was at or below the cost of capital.

Dominion's chairman and CEO was a guy called Tom Capps. We met him in London to discuss the proposed bid. He was a very loud American who clearly was not particularly focused on regulation issues and who wanted to buy a UK power company because that was what some of his peers were doing, and if that was the case then it must be the right thing to do. We further concluded – because he spoke about this at length – that he was an Anglophile who was attracted to the prospect of coming to Britain regularly. He kept talking about how his wife loved to go to Wimbledon, and he apparently spent two or three months of the year travelling around the UK, shooting game birds.

We did the deal and on completion in December 1996, I thought it appropriate that he should meet some of the local MPs, so we arranged a meeting on the terrace of the Houses of Parliament. Four or five of them came along, including Paddy Tipping, the left-wing Labour MP for Sherwood. He turned up wearing a sports jacket with badges down both lapels for everything from the National Union of Mineworkers to CND Ban the Bomb. Tom Capps went up to him, ignoring all these warning signs, and started a conversation. I was standing a few yards away and could hardly keep a straight face, because what Capps said was: "You're from Sherwood Forest – I think I have shot in your forest." Tipping gave him a death stare – Sherwood constituency was mainly a council housing estate. I dragged Capps away.

Anyway, Dominion's advisers then invited us to the celebratory dinner that is always held after a bid by the successful team. Of course, if the battle has been hostile, then the other side is never invited, but because this was all agreed, we got an invitation. I foolishly accepted it – the first and last time I ever made that mistake. It's something you should never do, go to somebody else's celebratory dinner when they have bought your business. Prizes were given out to various people involved – most of them were celebrating how clever they had all been. It was nauseatingly sycophantic and I sat there biting my tongue, because I knew that the winners were actually the East Midlands Electricity shareholders who had got a great price, and all the advisers who had trousered enormous fees.

As I suspected, Tom Capps discovered quite soon that East Midlands wasn't a great deal and like other American utilities that bought into the UK, Dominion sold out within two years. EME was then bought by PowerGen, one of the privatised British generating companies, which was allowed at that time to integrate vertically. PowerGen in turn was later acquired by E.ON, the huge German utility. In fact, almost the whole of the privatised electricity industry ended up in overseas hands.

That was the end of my first chairmanship outside the Williams orbit. It was something of a special case – for one thing, it was different from almost all my other chairmanships because I had never intended to become chair of EME and therefore faced a number of unexpected situations. It was not, of course, the last time that I had to deal as chairman with unpleasant surprises, but I took almost all my other non-executive positions either as chairman or with a commitment to become chairman.

Nonetheless, certain disciplines that I first applied at EME proved very valuable. One was the combination of financial and commercial nous I had developed through the Williams years and which in turn informed another extremely important competence: the ability to grasp quickly both the strategic and operational issues that a company was facing. Once I had done that, a number of important judgments invariably followed – not least the question of whether the CEO I had inherited was the right person to handle those issues.

At the outset, my skill set was not complete – I made very sure that I learned from the experiences that I accumulated as a chairman. But these fundamental principles stayed with me; and because they were universally relevant, they could be applied to a company in almost any line of business, in manufacturing or service sectors. They formed the bedrock of my non-executive career.

8

Pilkington

Having cut my teeth on EME, I was approached by Spencer Stuart again, this time in the shape of David Kimbell, about the glass-maker Pilkington. David was seen in the industry at the time as the great expert on non-executive directorships and was responsible for a large proportion of the appointments in the FTSE 100 and beyond.

David asked if I would agree to be put forward as a candidate to succeed the current chairman Sir Antony Pilkington, who seven years earlier had fought off a very acrimonious takeover bid by BTR. The new chairman would be the first from outside the company's founding family, which made it interesting from the start. Antony Pilkington, who was a true patrician, had been chairman since 1980 and was particularly keen to have someone from a place other than London on the board – he was very committed to England's industrial heartland and one of the reasons he chose me was that I was from the Midlands.

I joined the board in August 1994, and the plan was for me to take over as chairman the following July. However, before that happened I started asking difficult questions and there was a certain move on the board for me not to be appointed chairman. One of the directors involved was Sir Robin Nicholson, the government's former chief scientific adviser. I think all this made me keener to do the job, although I had serious reservations about the state of the business.

To understand the kind of company Pilkington was requires a bit of history. It was a family business, based in St. Helens, Lancashire, until 1960, when it was listed on the stock market. Over the years, it had bought a number of businesses to extend its international presence in glass manufacturing. One was Libby Owens Ford in the US, which was predominantly a supplier of automotive glass to General Motors. There was Flachglas in Germany, and a joint venture with Saint Gobain, its French peer, which virtually controlled both the auto and window glass market in South America. It also had a very interesting joint venture in China called SYP.

The glass industry had been revolutionised in the 1960s by Sir Alastair Pilkington, a brilliant Cambridge-educated engineer who invented the float glass manufacturing process. Sir Alastair was no relation of the Pilkington family – the fact that he had the same surname was one of those historical coincidences. It rather amused me, looking at one of the books that had been written about the company, to see in the family tree that there was no connection to him except for a footnote saying that he came from a different branch of the family. Pilkington had had all sorts of genealogists and people scouring archives to try to get a connection, but they had all failed – because there wasn't one.

Before Sir Alastair's breakthrough, high-quality glass could only be made by the so-called plate process, which was costly and created large amounts of waste material through grinding and polishing. Sheet glass was cheaper but, because it was not ground or polished, could not be used for high-quality applications like shop windows, vehicles or mirrors. In Pilkington's float glass process, a continuous ribbon of glass from a melting furnace is floated on the surface of a bath of molten tin, at a high enough temperature to melt all irregularities. Because the surface of the tin is flat, the glass also becomes flat – hence the name. The end product had uniform thickness and bright, fire-polished surfaces – so, no need for grinding and polishing.

The story goes that Sir Alastair got the idea when he was in the bath – a bit like Archimedes, although we don't know if he shouted "Eureka!" But it was certainly a life-changing moment for the company, transforming them at a stroke from a domestic British business into the technological world leader. It took seven years and a vast amount of money for Pilkington to make the process work: an extraordinary feat which almost bust the company, but eventually they succeeded. And they took out all the patents they needed to protect their intellectual property.

However, they were under-capitalised and therefore couldn't afford to open up wholly-owned plants around the world, which would have allowed them to really take advantage of the discovery and to secure its commercial benefits for the very long term. Instead, Pilkington created a global licensing network: in Japan, it licensed the process to Nippon Sheet Glass (NSG) and Asahi Glass; in the US to PPG (Pennsylvania Plate Glass), and so on in other territories. The royalty income from this network was huge and dwarfed any profit Pilkington made from its own glass business.

The fundamental problem that I eventually perceived was that the licensing strategy had made the company both an inefficient and a lazy business. It took me more than a year to realise this, because there were two things that I didn't do during the due diligence that I conducted before agreeing to become chairman: I didn't talk to the auditors or to the principal clearing bankers. I learned the hard way never to omit those discussions again.

When I did first meet the auditors privately, after becoming chairman, they confided that the company hadn't turned a profit out of making glass for at least a decade. All the money had come from the licensing royalties together with exchange rate gains (the pound had fallen against other currencies for much of this period) and other sorts of non-operating gains. Therefore, in their view the business had structural issues.

That was a worrying discovery, but the next thing was actually quite frightening. Roger Leverton, Pilkington's chief executive, and I were asked to meet the main syndicate of banks, who made it very, very clear to us that next time we wanted to roll over our facilities, this was going to be difficult because they considered that the business was badly run and cost-inefficient, and they wanted change. And they gave me six months to make that change.

The inefficiency stemmed from the fact that, because of float glass, Pilkington prided themselves on being the number one technologically and believed they needed to constantly prove that leadership. So, with every new float line they developed, they wanted to improve on the process again. As a result, everyone of their float lines was different and there was no standardisation – whereas their competitors took the Pilkington process and standardised it. As a result, these companies – Saint Gobain, PPG, Guardian – a US private company – and the Japanese became lowest-cost producers: they were producing float glass at about half the price of Pilkington, which was losing out in the marketplace.

But Pilkington was still getting the royalty income from licensing its patents to these competitors, and this was where the lazy element of the corporate culture kicked in. Instead of changing their manufacturing strategy to cut production costs and regain profitability, Pilkington became increasingly reliant on the royalties to generate its profits and dividends.

The problem came when the patents started to expire and therefore the royalty income began to fall. This was the point – in late 1986 – when the bid attack came in from BTR. BTR offered almost £1.2 billion for the company and Antony Pilkington put up an emotional, effective and well led (by Schroders) defence. Pilkington was also helped by a dramatic change in the UK political climate at the time – BTR's attack followed several other big hostile takeover battles and this sparked a temporary reaction against aggressive bids. Sir Owen Green, BTR's managing director, thought Pilkington was worth 700 pence a share at most. The political hostility did not mean that BTR could not succeed, but it raised the stakes so that BTR would have to pay a lot more. Their board decided that the new price of victory was too high, so they withdrew.

The problem was that Pilkington shares never again came near the price they reached during the BTR bid – 710 pence. However, I don't think BTR fully understood how difficult the business was. It was operating in areas where, particularly in auto glass, the vehicle manufacturers were pushing down prices and, as I have said before, the plants that Pilkington ran were high cost.

Pilkington did bizarre things to mitigate this. The technology the Japanese had in auto glass was the best in the world, and Pilkington decided to sell a percentage of Triplex, their auto glass business in the UK, to Nippon Sheet Glass (NSG) in exchange for the Japanese putting their management and technical expertise into the business to try and drive down costs in order to be competitive. So Pilkington ended up with NSG sitting in an important subsidiary as a significant shareholder, which caused all sorts of problems in transfer pricing of the glass and so on. It was a mess.

Even so, the Triplex deal was not the worst of their problems. Nothing can undermine a company so deeply as a big, bad acquisition – which was exactly what Pilkington had done. I believe the City was partly culpable for this. Having beaten off BTR, Pilkington were told by investors and analysts to get some growth into the business. They were then persuaded by Goldman Sachs – yes, them again – to diversify by buying VisionCare, a contact lens business owned by the cosmetics group Revlon. The price was sky-high at £361 million – and Pilkington financed it through a big rights issue.

The only similarity between Pilkington's glass business and VisionCare was that both made products that you looked through. The markets they served, the technology involved, everything else was different. So it was not a business Pilkington knew or understood. And if that wasn't bad enough, it was a hard lens business bought just before the entire market moved to soft lenses. Within months, it became apparent that they had bought an absolute pup. They not only lost the whole acquisition costs in terms of the value of the business, but the ongoing losses were enormous as well. And this put Pilkington in a dreadful position: they had spent a fortune on a terrible business and their core business was high-cost and low-margin with its patents and therefore royalty income running out.

After my revealing conversations with the auditors and the bankers, I started to get to grips with the business. I travelled round the country and round the world – South America, North America, mainland Europe – and saw the operations. And by any stretch of the imagination, these were very impressive: huge sites, making a beautiful product. But I couldn't understand how all this investment produced so little cash, and I then realised that it was because there were continued price-downs in the industry and, being the high-cost producer, Pilkington was always going to struggle.

One of my visits turned out to be particularly significant. A few years earlier, Pilkington had bought a 50% stake in a company called SIV, which was the Italian national glass manufacturer and almost entirely dedicated to supplying auto glass to Fiat, Renault and other European car makers. Pilkington's partner and owner of the other 50% was the Italian company Techint, which provided the top management for the joint venture. The man who ran it was Paolo Scaroni.

SIV had a plant in Venice which I visited, and I had dinner with Paolo. I was hugely impressed, not only with his knowledge of the business – he had previously worked for many years for Saint Gobain – but with his intelligence and charisma. He was a graduate of Milan's Bocconi University and Columbia in the States and was clearly a real business leader.

I started to compare him in my mind with Roger Leverton, and there was really no contest. Roger was a former Black & Decker and Rio Tinto executive who had been brought in several years earlier to shake things up. I'm a pretty good judge of people and whether they are being effective or not. In fact, I think that's my great strength.

As a chairman, I move round the business and just talk to people. I've always been good at that – basically because I enjoy doing it. Business is all about people and they tell me things that they might not tell someone more uptight, authoritarian or high-handed. I am honest with people. I've always tried to treat everyone with the same courtesy – unlike some leading business people I could name, I don't have one manner for the rich and powerful and another for the rest. For good or ill, what you see with me is what you get. Kipling wrote about walking with kings and not losing the common touch – I'm a great believer in that. He also had that great line about treating triumph and disaster as twin imposters – which is a message all industrialists should heed if they don't want to lose touch with reality.

Sometimes, the people I'm meeting don't even have to say anything: with the executive team, for instance, I can tell from the body language if there's a problem. It's intuitive. Luke Meynell of the head-hunter Russell Reynolds, whom I've known for many years, likens my approach to something his father, who was in the army and fought the communist guerrillas in Malaya in the 1950s, told him about that war. The British soldiers would be struggling through the jungle when their native trackers would suddenly tell them to lie down and not move. Within minutes, a bunch of the rebels would come past without seeing them. His father asked one of the trackers: "How do you know that the enemy is out there?" And the man said: "I've grown up in the jungle – you know something is wrong when the birds stop singing." Luke says I can sense in a company that the birds have stopped singing – that something is slightly off. As I said, it's a question of intuition.

You soon get to know how someone is reacting to your chief executive, what the relationships are, whether they are working well or not. I'm a great believer that, with a chief executive, you as chairman support him or her until you don't support them. There are certain chairmen who operate by starting to undermine a CEO's position. I don't play that game. I support until I decide a change is needed, and that is what I realised after some time at Pilkington. We were restructuring, but we weren't moving fast enough.

I therefore agreed to meet Paolo quietly in London a couple of weeks later, and we had a more in-depth conversation about Pilkington. I was nervous about the support I would get on the board for change, but I suggested to Roger Leverton that Paolo join the board as a kind of chief operating officer, to bring a knowledge of the glass business that I felt was lacking at the centre.

To my surprise, Roger agreed. I believe in his heart of hearts, he knew that he was out of his depth in the business, with all its problems. After a few months and some more poor results, I decided to move. I spoke to the board and said that I was very unhappy with the way Roger Leverton was running the business, and told them that I believed he was struggling. I thought he was a nice man, but that we had to make a change and I felt that Paolo Scaroni – if I could persuade him to come to the UK – would be the right person to run Pilkington: he knew the issues involved, the cost levels and all the rest of it, and he would deal with it.

The board agreed and I then flew over to Milan and had dinner with Paolo and his wife Francesca. I put it to him that we were minded to make him CEO in place of Roger. Paolo thought I was being very courageous since he had no experience of the UK or of British public companies. But I had no doubt that he was the right man for the job.

He then confided to me that he had one legacy issue. In the past, he had been involved in an industry-wide scandal to do with price-fixing in Italy, but that it had not been a major event and he had been one among many industrialists concerned. I therefore had to take a risk: Paolo had disclosed this to me and it was in the public domain. But I decided to go ahead because I felt so desperate that Pilkington needed new management and I thought Paolo was the right man. Sometimes you have to make a judgment and take the consequences. And in fact the issue was never raised by anyone.

The following Monday, I arranged to see Roger at Pilkington's London head office, a very grand building close to Buckingham Palace. I was frank: Pilkington needed urgent action and the board didn't believe Roger was the right man to provide it. I told him that, while I realised this would come as a blow to him, in time he would realise that the change was in his best interests as well as those of the company. He left the office and at my suggestion employed a good lawyer, and we agreed a severance package. He was a decent man who had been over-promoted and was ill-equipped to combat major problems that were historic and deep-seated. It wasn't all his fault: he had been working for a chairman who was a Pilkington, a lot of the board were old Pilkington people and one person trying to change an empire is quite difficult. You have to be very strong to do that, and Roger had made a big effort.

Paolo and I established an excellent relationship. I kept an office at Pilkington's London base but I was almost never there. Paolo, who has since become a chairman in his own right, appreciated this. "You are always there when I need you and never there when I don't," he said. Which is exactly how it should be. As he says, being a non-executive chairman is not a full-time job and if you get a chairman who transforms his or her job into a full-time one, then that person is always going to be treading on the toes of the CEO.

Luke Meynell once invited me to a chairman's lunch he was hosting – there were about eight of us there – and someone raised the subject of the chairman's office. One of the other guests said: "It's very important – I'm chairman of three companies and in each of them, I have an office marked 'chairman'." I couldn't resist responding, much to Luke's amusement, and said: "That sounds to me like terrible insecurity – the last thing a CEO wants is the chairman turning up next door on a regular basis." The other chap wasn't best pleased.

Where Paolo needed help was in acclimatising to the UK business world, so I took him under my wing, introduced him to a range of people in the City and industry, invited him to my club and took him shooting; we went out shopping one day and equipped him with all the necessary gear. Lesley and I invited him to our house many times, and later we went to the wedding of his daughter in Italy. "You were more than a chairman to me – more like a stepfather!" he told me once.

Paolo revitalised the business. He promoted some really good young people from within the company and he started to build better relations with our customers. He closed a number of businesses down: we were making double-glazing and all sorts of other glass products, all over the place, so he got rid of a lot of these activities. He also stopped a lot of the research and development that was nice to have, but which we could not afford.

One of Pilkington's problems was that they were always trying to find the next float glass, something that would lift them out of the ordinary world of selling glass and catapult them into a new world. This impulse was similar to their desire constantly to re-invent the process, which had driven up costs so much. One instance was that they spent a fortune on producing mirror glass on-line – in other words, in the same way that you made float glass.

They developed this novel process at huge expense without thinking about the real nature of the mirror glass industry, which for generations had been made in small plants which had probably been written off 30 years ago, and which were environmentally-unfriendly and therefore difficult to close down. They launched this product with great fanfare and of course what happened was that the existing manufacturers just dropped the price, because they could. So Pilkington's production became uneconomic.

Another example was self-cleaning glass. Great idea – wonderful to put on a new building because it cut the costs of window-cleaning at a later date. But again, it ignored the practical realities of how the market worked and what customers actually wanted. Building developers and renovators were not interested in paying a much higher cost for self-cleaning glass, for the simple reason that they themselves would not benefit from the saving on window-cleaners – the benefit would go to the tenants. So although it was a great product, successfully developed and still used, it was not a good business proposition and never took the market share that we wanted.

The business did improve remarkably under Paolo. We got the costs down where we could, we squeezed working capital and – very importantly - Paolo made a big impact in the City. He was a very open person, he knew all about the business and at the analyst presentations, he was superb. He became quite a star.

But he and I knew there was a limit. He was spending a lot of time away from home in the UK, working very long hours, and I often wondered how long he would be able to manage this. Then, one Friday in late May 2002, I was in Dornach in the north of Scotland playing golf with some friends and I got a call from Paolo. He said he had been asked by the Italian government to take over at Enel, the state-owned electricity giant. I said: "Well, Paolo, that is a bit of a shock. We are going to have to sort out a succession process over the next two or three months, and have an orderly handover."

He replied: "Nigel, you don't understand – the prime minister has personally asked me to do this job and he wants me to start on Wednesday next week!" All I could say, with typical British understatement, was: "Well, that is not very helpful."

I left my golf partners – I think we were on the tenth tee – and Sue managed to rent a private plane to go from Inverness airport to London. During the flight, I pondered what I should do. I had to decide very quickly: the timing dictated that it would almost certainly have to be an internal appointment, because if we went outside it would leave us in limbo for months while we found someone, and the company could not afford that. Despite all Paolo's great work, Pilkington was still not out of the woods.

We had some very good, young managers but one of them stood out: Stuart Chambers, who had joined as marketing director from Mars and had previously worked at Shell. At various management conferences I had attended, I saw that he was clearly somebody highly intelligent and prepared to ask difficult questions. I had marked him out as a star of the future, and Paolo had earmarked him as his eventual successor. However, Stuart was very young and, in my opinion, not truly ready to take on the chief executive's job. But I really had no choice.

I telephoned the other NEDs, who agreed with my conclusion, and then rang Stuart. He was in a management meeting at St. Helens and I asked him to come down to head office in London that evening. Selwyn House, the head office, was a very elegant building a few yards from St. James's Palace overlooking Green Park. When he got to my office that Friday night, I said: "Stuart, I have some good news and some bad news for you. The good news is that I would like you to take over as chief executive of Pilkington. The bad news is that you have to start next week. We haven't got time

110

to sort out a contract so you are going to have to trust me. I want your answer in the next couple of days."

I also suggested that he and his wife Nicky travel down from their home in Wilmslow to our house in Derbyshire for Sunday lunch, where we could discuss the situation more fully. I just wanted to make sure that Stuart's wife was up for the changes that were going to take place in their lives. We had a great lunch, and he agreed to do the job. The next day, we made what seemed in the City to be a seamless announcement that, after five years as Pilkington chief executive, Paolo was leaving to run Enel and Stuart Chambers was going to take over.

Paolo stayed on the Pilkington board as deputy chairman, and he remains a friend. I have the highest regard for him, but of course he put me in a very, very difficult position – I've never had to deal with anything like that before or since. Happily, Stuart did a tremendous job and proved that I made absolutely the right decision in promoting him. And it was never easy for him – Pilkington remained a company with very significant problems and its share price continued to languish.

Stuart ran the business for more than three years and during that time, we continued to have contact with the senior management of Nippon Sheet Glass. Because of the transfer pricing issues caused by NSG's stake in Triplex, we had decided during Paolo's tenure to simplify the whole structure by exchanging that Triplex shareholding for one in the parent company, so NSG ended up with 20% of Pilkington.

We got a sense that NSG wanted to own the iconic name that was Pilkington, and that they were prepared to pay almost any price. And eventually, NSG did indeed express an interest in buying the whole company. I was acutely aware that Pilkington was seen by politicians and the media as a major UK institution. But the board and I also knew that it was seriously challenged. We could continue to struggle along, but there was no top-line growth and little dividend growth, and it was very difficult to see how we could change that reality.

Pilkington was a classic case of a company that had lost so much ground in the world market and was weighed down by so much legacy debt that it could not recover. Despite all the self-help measures that we had taken, it was ultimately trapped in a spiral of decline. And it's very difficult for a company in that position to be able to break out. I've seen it done during my career, but very rarely. Much more often, the situation ends in a takeover and/or break-up.

The City recognised the position – our depressed share price was light years away from the BTR takeover bid days. And in late October 2005, when the shares stood at about 127p, NSG made a formal takeover approach. We negotiated, and the following February agreed a cash offer of 165p which valued Pilkington's equity at £2.2 billion (and, because it had £1.2 billion of net debt and pension obligations, gave it an enterprise value of £3.4 billion). The board and I felt that this was a full and fair price for the business. NSG not only committed to retain the Pilkington name and the St. Helens operation, but they also kept Stuart and his management team, who ended up running the whole group.

NSG never recovered from taking on the huge amount of debt they needed for the acquisition. They were still mired in debt for years afterwards and effectively became a zombie company. Operationally, they ran into the same problems that we wrestled with, coming under unrelenting pressure from the auto manufacturers on glass prices. Who knows what would have happened to Pilkington as an independent company – my guess is that it would either ultimately have been sold for a fraction of the price that I obtained, or it would have become a zombie company itself, or it would actually have gone out of business. Therefore, I have absolutely no doubt that the difficult decision to sell was the right decision.

I have applied similar criteria to every other bid I've received in my career. My fundamental priority is shareholder value. I know that's now a little old-fashioned since people talk about all sorts of stakeholders, national interest, etc. But I was brought up in a time when, as a director and chairman of a business, you focused on creating shareholder value. The best way to do that is to grow the business. But if somebody else comes along and offers a price for the company that gives you the right premium, then you have to consider it very seriously.

It's not a straight line – you don't just run up a *For Sale* flag. You might have to make two or three moves that open up your options. Invensys was a very good example. If you do get a bid, my rule of thumb has always been to look at the final offer price and then judge whether we can get to that share price within three years. If the answer is no, then you should accept the offer unless there is a very exceptional reason for not doing so. If you have a pretty successful business and think you have a decent chance of reaching the offer price within my timescale, then that's fine – reject the bid. But if it's a business that's hugely challenged, you have to do something that will save as much value for the shareholders as you can.

Pilkington was hugely challenged and NSG offered a 39% premium to its price immediately before the bid approach. With the pressures the business was under, I could not see Pilkington shares getting close to NSG's price, not just within three years, not ever. So although the external factors – the political and media sentiment – made the decision tough, in pure value terms I was absolutely clear that the decision to accept was correct. I haven't always been complimentary about City analysts in my career, but on the day that we announced NSG, at least one of them recognised that the takeover was "a great deal for Pilkington shareholders."

Stuart Chambers became chief executive of the whole of NSG and did an excellent job, but after several years based in Japan he had had enough of all the travelling, as well as the cultural attitude to business there, and he returned to the UK. Back here, he has had a very successful career as a chairman, first at the semiconductor company ARM Holdings and Rexam, the beverage can producer, and latterly at the miner Anglo-American and Travis Perkins, the building products distributor. I made absolutely the right decision in promoting him, although I wouldn't want to repeat the timing involved – and fortunately I have never had to. One of the chairman's most important and hardest tasks is to ensure the company has the right chief executive, and that normally demands careful and patient consideration. Stuart was the exception to that rule.

With Prince Charles

9

Boots

Boots was based in Nottingham and a pillar of East Midlands industrial life, so I was immediately receptive when, in 1999, I was asked by the head-hunter Anna Mann if I would be interested in joining the board. At the time, this was just to become a non-executive director, not as a prelude to taking over as chairman.

On the face of it, this seemed like quite a good idea – I was still chairman of Williams, Pendragon and Pilkington but I could see that Williams might be drawing to a close. And in those days, investors were more interested in whether a NED was experienced and competent than in how many directorships they had or how long they had sat on a particular board.

Boots was then dominated by Lord (James) Blyth, who had been chief executive since 1987 and had subsequently become chairman as well. Executive chairmen were still accepted in the City then, as long as they had a decent track record. After a difficult start, Blyth was seen to have done a reasonable job and I met him and the rest of the board. I knew Bob Gunn, one of Blyth's predecessors as chairman who had been on the East Midlands Electricity Board with me, and I discussed the business with him.

I concluded that joining the board would be rather interesting, so I accepted the invitation and had a couple of board meetings with Lord Blyth in the chair. In mid-2000, he then stepped down after Anna Mann arranged an unusual swap of roles with John McGrath, chairman of the drinks group Diageo. Blyth became chairman of Diageo and McGrath joined Boots as chairman.

I had three years as a NED, during which I got to know the business thoroughly and came to understand the significant issues that it faced. Many people in the City were describing Boots in somewhat uncomplimentary terms as a legacy retailer. The sharpest refrain was that if Boots didn't exist, you wouldn't invent it.

To understand how Boots had arrived at the point where analysts were basically wondering if it would survive in the twenty-first century, you probably need to go back a bit. The company was founded in the mid-nineteenth century by John Boot, an apothecary in Nottingham, and expanded by his son Jesse and his wife, who started to make cosmetic products available in the stores. Dramatic growth took place in the early twentieth century, when Boots went from nothing to opening about 1,000 stores nationwide and became a household name. It became a public company but was still controlled by the Boots family, and in 1920 was bought by United Drug Company from Boston in the US for $10 million. United Drug sold it during the Depression by floating it back on the London Stock Exchange in 1933 under John Boot, Jesse's son.

There it stayed, expanding from retailing into a fully-fledged pharmaceutical business through heavy research and development spending which during the 1960s led Boots scientists to develop ibuprofen. However, its prescription drugs business had declined by the early 1990s and was sold to Germany's BASF. The profitable legacy of the pharma operation was some leading over-the-counter brands including Nurofen and Strepsils.

Boots' head office on the outskirts of Nottingham occupied 300 acres and resembled a university campus. As I attended various board meetings, I used to see huge numbers of people in various meeting rooms and I observed that the whole company seemed to be highly bureaucratic. This perception was confirmed when I talked to suppliers, who said Boots was an extremely loyal customer, but that dealing with the company was a nightmare because all new products and new ideas took ages to market, since so many people were involved in the decision-making process.

The biggest problem of all was that footfall in the stores had been declining for many years. Boots' first response was to keep prices high, relying on their customers' loyalty, while seeking new streams of income. It was universally known as Boots the Chemist, but it changed its name to The Boots Group to reflect its diversification strategy. This led Blyth – shortly after becoming CEO – to take over the Ward White retail group, which included a DIY chain (Do-It-All) and Halfords, the car and bike accessories chain. Do-It-All cost them an estimated £400 million over nine years before it was sold, although Halfords did well.

When I joined the board, the company had an odd management structure with joint managing directors, one being Steve Russell, who headed the chemist business. He knew that business very well, being a lifetime Boots employee who had worked in the company as a pharmacist. He had also played county cricket for Nottinghamshire. The other managing director was David Thompson, the finance director who really ran the company.

While reversing the previous strategy of diversifying into completely unrelated businesses like DIY, they had embarked on a process of using spare space in the chemist stores, particularly in town centres where many shops had an upstairs floor that was little used by customers. They converted these floors into locations for physio, dental, health and beauty and other quasi-medical services – at one point, Boots was the biggest buyer of dental equipment in Europe, and possibly in the world.

None of these new services made money, partly because the way Boots operated in dentistry was to employ dentists on a salary basis. Most people who understand the business realise that dentists are usually paid according to output, and it was my opinion that Boots attracted just about every lazy dentist in the country! But they operated with the finest equipment, so not surprisingly the business ran at a loss.

The management structure changed when Lord Blyth left, with

John McGrath becoming non-executive chairman and Steve Russell chief executive. In 2003, after three years, McGrath decided to retire because of ill health and I was asked by the board to become chairman. I made it very clear that a condition of my acceptance would be the recruitment of a new CEO. The board approved this change and I agreed to become chairman: Steve Russell was a very nice guy, but he was not tough enough and in fact he agreed with my decision.

I led the search for the new CEO, interviewing a number of people including Justin King, who later became CEO of Sainsbury's. There was someone from Homebase and then there was Richard Baker, who was Deputy CEO of Asda.

I met Richard, who gave me his strong view that Boots was a healthcare company which had lost its way and had turned itself into a department store, and that it should go back to doing what it did best. This obviously struck a chord with me and I arranged to meet him again. He came to my home at midday on a Sunday – we actually had a party for the grandchildren going on, and every so often we were interrupted by a child running into the room waving a tomahawk and wearing a head dress, which Richard found slightly surreal. But I learned a lot about him and I liked what I learned.

His father was a Midlands industrialist from Sutton Coldfield, near Birmingham, and Richard had studied engineering at Cambridge before joining Mars, which was renowned as an excellent training-ground for management. He was also highly ambitious – he had set himself the goal of running a company by the time he was 40. Which was about now.

That was good to hear, because it told me he had drive and determination, but what really impressed me was Richard's analysis of Boots. Richard said, correctly, that the company had become fat and uncompetitive. His plan was 'to put the Chemist back into Boots and make Boots *the* Chemist.' As Asda's deputy CEO, he was running all its commercial activities and he had noted that, every time they launched some marketing initiative in health and beauty, Tesco would match it within a week. Boots simply did not react.

The Asda people thought that they must be asleep in Nottingham. Richard said Boots should shed the peripheral activities and focus on healthcare, where it was still a fantastic brand.

With Richard Baker, CEO of Boots – and a classic car!

Since this was exactly what I had concluded, we were on the same page from the start. The attempt to move away from the core business had been a complete failure. Boots' prices were too high, we were losing market share and we would have to take a hit to sort it all out. That would require both expertise and resolve.

It was immediately clear that he was the best person to take the business forward, and so I asked the head-hunter to set up meetings for him over the next couple of weeks with some of the other non-executive directors. Those went fine. I then asked him to come to Williams' Derby office, where I offered him the job and asked him what it would take to persuade him to accept. He replied: "Not very much, because I really want this job." And we agreed to get the head-hunter to establish the average rate for this kind of CEO position. Richard was happy to accept that. We had a short chat and in 20 minutes we had come to an agreement.

I wanted to have one final talk with him, so I asked him to see me the Sunday before he started. We arranged to meet at a hotel in Sheffield – I drove up from Derby and Richard came down from his home near Leeds. Again, the setting was slightly incongruous because there was a wedding going on. It was a lovely afternoon, so we found a bench in the garden while the wedding reception was taking place a few yards away from us across the lawn.

I told him that I had three rules for the way the chairman and the CEO work together. The first was that we did not do each other's jobs – the chairman ran the board and the CEO ran the company. I would not step on his toes. Rule two was that bad news travels fast but good news can wait. In other words, if there was anything untoward – be it a warehouse fire, an imminent profit warning or a nasty piece in the *Sunday Times* – the first thing Richard should do is to call me and rule one would come into play: if it was a board matter, I would deal with it; if the problem related to operations, I would expect Richard to tell me what he was going to do about it.

Then I told him the third and final rule. "I'll back you," I said, "until I sack you." This startled Richard and he exclaimed: "Whoa – I'm only starting tomorrow and you are talking about sacking me already. I know you've got a reputation, but I wasn't expecting to hear that this quickly!"

I explained that, "There will never be a moment where you doubt my support – until there's a moment where I can no longer give you that support. That may never happen, but if it does, then you and I will have a straightforward, polite and gentlemanly conversation and you will leave the company." Richard has told me since that, as chairman of his own companies, he has a similar conversation about the three rules with all his new CEOs.

He and I struck up a great working relationship from the start and I made sure that everyone in the company realised we were standing shoulder to shoulder – literally, in one instance. We knew that stemming the company's decline was going to be difficult. There was no quick fix and there would be quite a lot of pain. Richard and his executive team put together a turnround plan, we got Christmas trading out of the way, and then Richard announced a pretty savage redundancy programme. We knew that this would shock our people, who were used to the comfort of the old, paternalistic culture. It would also have ramifications for the city of Nottingham, where Boots was just about the largest employer and cast a long shadow. Almost everyone was related to someone or knew someone who worked, or had worked, there.

The announcement was therefore a critical moment in our turn-round effort. Richard called together the 3,000 people in head office and stood on the balcony above the assembly to tell them that one in three jobs had to go. I knew that the choreography here was very important, because it would send a powerful message. Richard of course had the executive team standing behind him on the balcony, and I was there too. While he was speaking, I deliberately stepped forward and stood just behind his right shoulder. Then, when he had finished, I stepped back. Richard was not even aware that I was alongside him for those moments, but no-one on the floor below was left in any doubt that he had the full support of the chairman and that together, we were totally committed to making the strategy a success.

Boots had become very dependent on consultants, which was not healthy. One of them, for instance, had a very strange methodology in which he analysed just about every product we sold and tried to work out if it was value-creative or value-destructive. This produced some bizarre answers: he decided the selling of nappies was a value destroyer, because the margin was small. This completely ignored the fact that having nappies on the shelves brought people into the stores, where they bought other products.

David Thompson in particular had become heavily reliant on consultants and used them almost as a crutch rather than making decisions himself. I told him before he retired that I was very unhappy with the way consultants were effectively running the business. I said that, if we didn't have the management to run it ourselves, we should employ people who could. David Thompson's successor as finance director was Howard Dodd, who was appointed before Richard came in and who left a couple of years later as we built a new management team.

Richard and I found it hard going. I used to have a sandwich lunch with him every Monday so that he could update me about what was happening in the business, what decisions were coming up, what was going to be on our agenda for the next board meeting. One Monday, about six months in, he turned up looking worn out.

I told him, "Richard, you look knackered!" To which he replied, "You got that in one – this is really tough."

I said, "I know – welcome to the real world!"

It was banter – we always agreed that it was important to find something to laugh about in difficult situations – but with a serious undertone. Inevitably, given the scale of the turnround task, it was taking its toll. So I asked him: "Who's running your Fridays?" He asked me what I meant and I said: "A CEO should never have anything in their diary on a Friday. You have to have a thinking day. If you are tearing round with your tail on fire every day, when are you going to do your thinking?" Then I called out to Sue: "Can you ring Nottingham Golf Club – Richard and I are playing golf 10.00 am Friday morning."

Richard went back to his office and cleared his diary for that Friday. We had a great round – four hours of fresh air, sunshine and talking over lots of stuff. Richard joked: "I came from Mars, so I believe in Work, Rest and Play!" He told Kim, his PA, not to put any meetings in the diary for future Fridays, and he says that, to this day, he has never again had a Friday business meeting.

We had at least one profit warning in the first year, the media was bad and shareholders were becoming very unhappy with what was happening. We bit the bullet and took down our prices, which obviously destroyed margin and profitability and was disliked by the analyst community. But we thought that it was imperative to reset and to halt the loss of market share.

However, the negative sentiment was of course feeding back into the business. As Richard put it, it seemed to many people that we were taking two steps forward and two – sometimes three – steps back. About a year after we announced the strategy, we had a store managers' conference – there were about 1,800 managers. During the day, Richard and his team made presentations and after the dinner, I stood up and made a short speech.

In some situations with some of the companies I've headed, this kind of thing is just a formality – the chairman turns up and delivers a few pleasantries to help send everyone home in good spirits. This was very different. People knew my reputation for hiring and firing CEOs. It was a bit like the chairman and the football manager – people in the company were starting to ask, "How many more games has this guy got?" So I stood up and said: "I want you all to know that Richard and I started this project together, and we will finish this project together." Richard has told me since how much he appreciated that – for our managers, it was a hearts and minds moment, and crucial that they should see we were in total solidarity.

Pharmacy was our core business. The previous management had lost faith in it and therefore lost sight of that basic fact. The other jewels in Boots were some of their own brands. The No.7 brand was the leading cosmetic brand in the country. In fact, the margins on the No.7 brand alone accounted for a very, very large proportion of profits. And we also had a number of generic products such as Nurofen, which were highly profitable. We decided to divest Nurofen and some of the other over-the-counter products. We sold them to Reckitt Benckiser for almost £2 billion and then handed £2 a share in cash to our long-suffering shareholders, which was the first decent return of capital that they had received in years.

Boots had some retail businesses overseas – Thailand, the Netherlands, Japan – which they had tried to grow but, as numerous British store chains have learned the hard way, national retailers in general do not travel well because other parts of the world do not understand them. Maybe there are some world brands, but generally speaking retail is very much a local thing. Boots had lost huge amounts of money in Japan, where they had spent heavily on flagship stores in Tokyo and so on. We really had to cut all this out, so we closed the overseas operations.

With all these actions to eliminate loss-makers and sell profitable non-core interests, we got the business back on a stable footing. Certainly the private shareholders seemed to recognise our efforts – they continued to turn up in numbers at our annual general meeting, and they never gave me a rough ride. One of them even contributed the most memorable – and amusing – question that I've ever fielded at an AGM.

Most AGMs are uneventful, and if you keep a good grip on the agenda, you can get them over and done with pretty quickly. I have never experienced as chairman a really rough event, although as a NED I have been present at one or two. The Barclays and BAE Systems meetings were seriously challenging at times and I was quite pleased to be an observer on those occasions.

I've dealt with all sorts of questions from shareholders when chairing AGMs, some of them relevant and the occasional one a real surprise. But nothing quite like this one at a Boots meeting, when an elderly gentleman stood up and addressed me.

"My wife died last month," he said. Then he paused, and I remember thinking that maybe we had made a mistake on her prescription and wondered if what was coming next might be news of a lawsuit. Not a bit of it. "I wanted to know," the recently-bereaved shareholder inquired, "whether it is possible to transfer her Advantage Points to me, or do they cancel out on death?"

I had very rarely been lost for words while chairing an AGM, but this time I did struggle for a response, particularly as I was desperately trying not to burst out laughing – as one or two of the other shareholders had. Eventually, I suggested to him that, after the meeting, he should talk to our customer service desk who would look into the issue. Nothing at an AGM ever surprised me after that.

After two years of very hard slog, our underlying performance was improving and the share price began to respond. However, the fundamental challenge that Richard and I had to respond to remained: how to get long-term growth out of the core pharmacy business. We had several options. We could throw in the towel and sell to private equity; we could keep Boots public and run it for cash, paying good dividends and doing share buybacks – but that wouldn't do anything to grow the business and would make it very difficult to attract good people to work for us. Or we could play to our name as a pharmacy business and buy into Europe, which was the obvious geographical market to enter. What we needed was a partner in mainland Europe.

Here, my Pilkington position played a key role. When I joined the board of Boots, Paolo Scaroni had introduced me to Stefano Pessina, who had created one of the leading European wholesale pharmacy groups, Alliance Unichem. Paolo was chairman of the company, and he invited me to Rome to have dinner with Stefano, and we got on well. Subsequently, I had lunch with Stefano a couple of times in London and I learned a bit more about his business.

Alliance Unichem had started with a pharmacy wholesale business in Naples owned by the Pessina family. Stefano was a nuclear physicist by training but was asked by the family, I think on the death of his father, to take over running the business. His philosophy and how he grew the operation was first to analyse the various markets for drug distribution in Europe. They were very local, usually being done by cooperatives in a particular town or area; pharmacists clubbed together to create buying groups in order to get best prices.

Stefano saw an expansion opportunity and explained to these chemists that they could get better value by selling their wholesale businesses to him, enabling him to use his increased scale and greater purchasing power with the manufacturers to get better prices for them. Over time, in Italy, France, Spain and Portugal he built the Alliance Group. Then he looked at the UK, where the big wholesale business was United Chemists. It had originally been owned by pharmacists who then floated it on the stock market as Unichem. Stefano agreed a takeover of the company and his business became Alliance Unichem (AU).

During our conversations, Stefano made no secret of his wish to own Boots. He thought it was a sleeping giant and he believed that the benefits of combining the buying power of Alliance Unichem and Boots, particularly in generic medicines, would be huge. I kept in touch with him, and in 2005 he formally approached me with the idea of merging the two companies. Paolo, who was party to the proposal, made it clear that if the deal went ahead, I would become chairman of the combined group and he would step down as chairman of AU.

I talked to Richard and he also thought that the combination made a lot of sense. AU was very high-growth, but also quite heavily indebted because of the acquisitions it had made to fuel its expansion. Boots was basically ex-growth, but had a very strong balance sheet with lots of cash and assets. We would be able to use the strength of the Boots balance sheet to reduce the debts and invest in the high-growth parts of the AU business. AU had just entered Russia and China – Boots was a domestic UK business.

We consulted the board and the senior executives. At first, there was a reluctance to engage. They believed Boots was a better business than AU, where analysts had demonstrated that a lot of its growth in profits had been bought through the acquisitions rather than generated organically. There was therefore a suspicion that its quality of earnings was lower than ours.

I understood this view, but I was also hugely impressed with Stefano's dynamism and his vision of a worldwide pharmacy business that would eventually encompass the US, South America and China. Stefano believed that merging Alliance and Boots would make that possible. Having got to know him, I saw that this was not pie in the sky. Stefano knew the industry inside out, had proved that he could internationalise and above all he was totally driven – perhaps the most driven person I've ever met in business.

We set up a number of working parties to examine the proposal from every angle. Increasingly, the answer came that it would be good for Boots. Our top 15 executives concluded that there was no downside – it would create a European pharmacy powerhouse.

After some really tough negotiations, we agreed on a merger and announced it.

I knew it would be a difficult sell to the City. The sell-side analysts didn't like it because they didn't understand the logic of creating an integrated European healthcare distributor and retailer. One of the problems was that Boots was covered by retail sector analysts and Alliance Unichem by Healthcare analysts – it's bizarre, but that's how the analysts were demarcated. The Boots analysts took the view that had been held initially by a number of people inside Boots, that Alliance Unichem was of lower quality than the Boots business and would dilute the franchise. My view was completely the opposite: I thought Boots was a great business, a fantastic brand name which was one of the most trusted in the UK – but I just couldn't see where we were going to get growth.

Merging with Alliance created value: it gave us substantial synergies through much greater scale in buying and it brought Stefano Pessina into the group. He joined the board as executive deputy chairman and through his large stake in Alliance became the combined group's biggest shareholder with about 15%. Richard remained CEO with me as chairman. Stefano's role was to head strategy.

We delivered the synergies that we promised – in fact, we over-delivered. And the City started to recognise the performance: when we merged, the market value of the combined business was about £7 billion and 18 months later it had risen to almost £8 billion with our shares at about £8, so we had a bit of momentum. Some analysts were starting to say that the share price could even hit £10. And when Richard did the post-results roadshows, investors were becoming receptive.

However, I thought that the City still didn't really take on board the vision that we had for the business to go worldwide. As a result, the share price had not reached a level where we could consider making some acquisitions in the US, where the kind of businesses we wanted to buy were more highly-rated. Stefano became increasingly impatient with the City's attitude and told me so. One Thursday afternoon, I was in our head office on Oxford Street when Stefano asked to see me. He gave me a piece of paper that said KKR, the big US private equity firm, advised by Merrill Lynch, wanted to take the company private. And he indicated that they were willing to pay £10 a share, which was a premium of about 25% to the undisturbed price.

The possibility of a bid had been at the back of my mind after what Stefano had said to me over the months. I called Richard, who was preparing to go to a long service awards dinner to make some presentations to employees. I said: "I need you to come to my home tomorrow afternoon. I can't tell you on the phone what it's about." I knew what Richard would immediately infer – when the chairman asks to see the CEO privately at very short notice, the CEO will conclude that he's about to be removed. So I said: "I know what you must be thinking and it's not that. But I can't say any more now. See you tomorrow."

When Richard arrived on the Friday, I told him: "You'll need to sit down for this." I handed him the paper that Stefano had given me and went to make us a cup of tea. Then we discussed the new situation.

One immediate issue was Stefano's position, which presented me with a huge dilemma. He was obviously conflicted immediately and I had to exclude him from any board discussions, but I didn't want to remove him from the company because he was quite important to its future, whatever happened.

We then entered discussions with KKR, whose team was led by Dominic Murphy and Henry Kravis, one of the firm's founders whom I had met many, many years before. We now became reacquainted. Even by their standards, what was being proposed was a very big deal – no FTSE 100 company had ever been through a 'take private' and this would be Europe's largest leveraged buy-out.

With our advisers, I went through the whole game of telling them the offer wasn't high enough, we needed more, etc. And in the end, they came up with a number – just under £11 – which I thought was a good price but not fantastic. However, our room for manoeuvre was limited because they initially seemed to be the only bidder in town.

We had excluded a number of people inside Boots from our discussions, but there was one person in particular who I kept on board even though I knew he was very close to Stefano and would relate all our discussions back to him. In fact, it was for that very reason that I kept this guy informed – I knew that if I wanted to send a message to Stefano at any stage, I could use this channel. And soon after the whole situation became public, I had occasion to do precisely that.

After we announced that we had this offer from KKR, I was approached by Guy Hands, founder of the PE firm Terra Firma, who was supported by the Wellcome Trust healthcare organisation. They wanted to make a counter-bid. This transformed the situation and created a tremendous opportunity for us to maximise shareholder value. Terra Firma were obviously the underdog because Stefano was in such a powerful position as a major shareholder, but they were a serious contender. We called a board discussion and before the meeting, knowing that our deliberations would leak back to Stefano, I privately warned the other board directors not to give any indication that we realised Stefano and KKR were strongly-placed.

Sure enough, within two days of our meeting, Stefano rang me to say that he had heard on the grapevine that there was another bid pending. He asked to meet me and I agreed. We met at my London home and I told him quite frankly that there was indeed another interested party and that KKR's offer was unsatisfactory. Stefano was in an interesting position. He had to win, otherwise he would be out of the business that he had built up. But he was seller as well as buyer, so he did not mind if KKR raised its bid – in fact, he effectively had an incentive for them to do so: his holding in Alliance Boots meant that the higher the purchase price, the more he would make on a takeover. So he was very relaxed about raising the offer. I asked him: "Can you persuade KKR to pay up?" And he said he could, because they were backing him. So he went back to KKR, they raised the offer to £11.39 a share and we accepted it, although Guy Hands was furious that we hadn't given him another opportunity to bid.

In the event, we got a very good price for the Alliance Boots share-holders. We had increased the group's value from £7 billion at the 2005 merger to the KKR buy-out price of just over £11 billion. That was a very full price by any reckoning, including my rule of thumb on takeover bids. At this point, my frustration with the City analysts boiled over and I told Beth Rigby, then the retail correspondent of the *Financial Times* and now political correspondent for Sky News, that the retail analysts had consistently undervalued Alliance Boots because they knew nothing about the value of a business. She rang me up afterwards and said: "I hope this isn't a Ratner moment for you" – referring to Gerald Ratner's infamous comment that one of his jewellery products was "total crap." It was considerate of her but I said: "I don't care about the analysts – I'm not going to go back into the retail sector anyway." And I never have done.

All that remained was to ensure that Richard and I received what I believed was fair reward for our efforts in driving the increase in shareholder value. All the executives gained from the take-out price through their share option schemes and as CEO, Richard was obviously the biggest beneficiary. But the way share option schemes work, the board always has a fair amount of discretion over the precise amounts that are paid out. I put a very strong case to the board that Richard should get the maximum that he was entitled to, and they accepted my submission.

As for me, in the public company world, all the chairman receives even after an exceptional event like this is to receive a flat fee which is unrelated to the result. So I requested an ex gratia payment and Richard backed my proposal. The board agreed and I immediately donated the money to the independent Derby Grammar School: my old school Bemrose had been turned into a comprehensive by the Labour government of the 1970s, and a group of old boys from the two former grammar schools in the city subsequently clubbed together to create this new independent school, of which I am patron.

Richard and I believed that Boots was going to a good home, and experience has borne out that judgment. It became part of the largest pharmacy group in the world. Had Boots remained by itself, it would have had to survive Covid-19 and carnage on the High Street – it could even have become a Debenhams or a House of Fraser.

Instead, Stefano took charge of the business and a few years later he engineered its acquisition by the big American pharmacy group Walgreens, eventually becoming its chief executive. It wasn't all plain sailing for what was called Walgreens Boots Alliance, but Stefano had realised his long-standing US ambition. I have got an enormous amount of admiration for him, although he is an absolute workaholic: he had a beautiful yacht in the Mediterranean but on the odd occasion when I was on it, he would spend hours poring over spreadsheets and budget forecasts. I used to think to myself, *What a waste!* I've always believed that business should be fun as well as hard work – otherwise what's the point – but Stefano didn't see it that way. Work is his life.

10

Barclays

I had been a business banking client and customer of Barclays for many years, since the early days of Williams. The relationship grew even closer when Williams became a client of BZW after Barclays founded the investment bank in 1986, and we had a great team on the account.

In 1995, around the time I started as chairman of Pilkington, I had a call from Andrew Buxton, Barclays' chairman. He asked if I would come and see him and his chief executive, Martin Taylor, because they had decided to appoint an industrialist to the board and they thought I might be the person they wanted.

I was amazed really. At that time, to be appointed to the board of one of Britain's largest banks was just about the top of the corporate tree. Today, you would run as fast and as far away from the job as your little legs would carry you, but that was a completely different world. To be a director of Barclays was a kind of pinnacle, and here was I, only 49 years old, being invited to become one. There was no process. Amazingly, I didn't meet any of the other directors. Andrew and Martin interviewed me and Andrew then said that they would like me to join the board, which I did. My appointment took effect on 1 February 1996.

My boardroom career at Barclays lasted 13 years, longer than anything I have been involved in in business outside Williams and Pendragon. I could not have done that in today's corporate governance-dominated world. But I certainly benefited enormously from what, by any standards, was a remarkable experience, and I would like to think that the perspective I brought to bear over those years also benefited the bank and its shareholders.

For the last five years or so of my tenure I was deputy chairman – senior independent director in today's parlance. During that time, I was twice asked to put my name forward as chairman, but I declined on both occasions because I believed that, for all the experience of banking that I had accumulated by then – which was a lot – the chairman of one of the world's major banks should be a banker. And I still believe that. Of course, it would have been quite something for Nigel Rudd from Derby, who never even went to university, to become chairman of Barclays. But one of the guiding principles of my business life has always been to make judgments and decisions as objectively as is humanly possible, and to take ego out of the equation. I've seen more than enough examples of the damage that business leaders driven by personal ambition can do to a company.

So I entered the Barclays boardroom and had my eyes opened very fast. The directors were an interesting group. At the time that I joined, Barclays was still recovering from the property crash of the early 1990s. Andrew Buxton, who had been chairman and chief executive during that period, was held responsible for a number of the bad deals they had done. As a result, investors had forced him to split the roles and appoint a CEO from outside the bank.

The board had chosen Martin Taylor, although his background might not have made him the most obvious candidate for the job. He was a former *Financial Times* journalist whose only CEO position had been at Courtaulds Textiles, the company created by the chemicals group Courtaulds when it broke itself up in 1990.

Martin's mentor was Sir Christopher Hogg, his former boss at Courtaulds. I had dealt with Chris Hogg when Williams was looking to expand in paints and we tried to buy Courtaulds' international paints business. Chris Hogg was very cerebral, an intellectual who was highly rated by business school academics, but I thought he didn't really have a great feel for business. He had come up through the Industrial Reorganisation Corporation (IRC), the body set up by Harold Wilson's government in the 1960s to restructure British industry. I don't know if his tenure at Courtaulds was hugely successful or not. The group was eventually taken over by AkzoNobel, but that was long after his time.

Martin Taylor was from exactly the same mould. At first, I didn't know what to make of him, but he had the same kind of intellectual demeanour as Chris Hogg. He also had a very high opinion of himself and, I thought, a low opinion of just about everybody else. He was one of the very few business leaders who spoke Mandarin, something which seemed to fascinate the media even though it was irrelevant to how he ran Barclays. They kept referring to him as being fluent in Mandarin. This media stuff reminded me of what someone said about the Labour MP who had to resign as a result of the House of Commons expenses scandal – "He knew five languages but he spoke nonsense in all of them." I'm not a great linguist and Martin didn't talk nonsense. But as far as I was concerned, the fact that he could speak Mandarin didn't automatically qualify him for anything. The only thing that mattered was whether he was a good CEO.

The board was certainly heavyweight. For a start, we had Lord Lawson, Thatcher's former chancellor, who made lots of speeches – he seemed to go on for hours and hours, and if the chairman tried to stop him, he just raised his voice and carried on with his particular monologue. We also had some really talented non-executives: I thought Sir Nigel Mobbs, chairman of Slough Estates (now Segro) who was the senior NED when I started, was fantastic. Lady Mary Baker, wife of the cabinet minister Lord (Ken) Baker, also stood out as somebody who was extremely sensible and who I learned a lot from.

Two months after I started, BZW suffered a huge blow when David Band, who had been its chief executive since it was created, died suddenly of a heart attack at the age of 53. That triggered a large number of changes at BZW. Bob Diamond, who eventually became Barclays' CEO, was appointed by Martin Taylor to head its fixed income division. And Bill Harrison, who was known throughout the City as 'Attila the Brum' because he came from Birmingham and was a hyperactive deal-maker, was made CEO of BZW. I knew Bill well because he was on the board of Pilkington for seven years when I was chairman, and I liked him very much. But anyone less suited to manage a big organisation I couldn't imagine. Bill was a seat-of-the-pants investment banker and putting him in charge of running BZW was simply wrong.

Martin Taylor's management style soon became an issue for me. At board meetings, it seemed to me that Martin showed no interest whatsoever in the views of the NEDs: he just ignored us. I think he genuinely believed that – apart from Lord Lawson, with whom he got on well - we had nothing to offer. According to Philip Augar in his recent book on Barclays (*The Bank That Lived a Little*), Taylor thought that we did not understand how investment banking was changing or what Barclays' 'real role in the world' was. If any of us raised issues, he showed bored irritation and made no effort at all to connect. In an effort to understand him better, I deliberately sat next to him at a board lunch; he refused to engage and demonstrated quite clearly what I had already surmised about his lack of interest in what NEDs thought. He seemed to see me as a northern oik, which was odd considering he was born in Burnley.

He was also reluctant to engage with us because Barclays suffered from recurrent leaks to the media, to the point where Martin complained that the board was leaking. Board leaks are always a by-product of an unhappy board. In an attempt to stop this, Martin brought in Control Risks, the security people, to interview all the NEDs, which didn't help our relationship with him. Sir David Arculus, who had built up the publishing group EMAP and later became chairman of O2, was particularly incensed. According to Augar, Taylor decided that he would share his thinking with us only when absolutely necessary.

Altogether, it was a very unhappy board and I very soon made it clear that I wanted to leave if the management style didn't change. As you can imagine, this didn't go down particularly well with the chief executive, and I was later told by a fund manager who seemed particularly well informed that Martin wanted to clear out the NEDs because he thought we were all useless. I have to admit that I was guilty of telling Jeff Randall, then editor of *Sunday Business*, that Martin was all brains and no judgment. Jeff kept the source confidential, attributing the comment to "someone close to the board." Unfortunately, it was an expression that I had used in a private session of the NEDs! I learnt a lesson and, despite my frustrations, kept my head down after that.

One of the main problems was that Andrew Buxton was a thoroughly decent man but I felt that, with the very difficult situations we had, he was out of his depth. Andrew was the last actual member of Barclays' founding families to have become chairman and CEO, but as chairman, he disliked confrontation. He didn't really handle Martin in terms of counselling him about NEDs and how to keep people on board with him, and he didn't always inform the NEDs of what was happening, either. Even taking into account the Chairman's ambassadorial role, he did not seem to be as involved with matters as he could have been. He also came under a lot of pressure from shareholders to step down, because some of them felt he was not up to the job.

The first really massive issue, which also highlighted the deficiencies of Martin Taylor's approach to the board, occurred in late September 1997, just over 18 months after I became a director. Martin decided to break BZW up and sell the investment banking business – the equities and corporate finance side. I was only a junior board member at this stage, but I was very, very angry about the way the sale was handled. The decision was sprung on the board and I knew enough about corporate governance to call Andrew Buxton to ask for an emergency board meeting. I told Andrew that we should have had the opportunity to discuss the plan properly instead of being put in a position where we had to accept what was effectively a fait accompli.

It had been very clear to me that Martin did not like BZW because of its lack of good returns and the risk inherent in the model. The problem was that the board had never had a decent discussion about a sale. And he had no concept of the planning needed to sell a business, particularly a business like that. He is on record as saying that he acted the way he did because he didn't trust the board. But the board didn't trust him and the whole thing became a nightmare.

In fact, Martin may well have been right about BZW. Barclays created it because, with Big Bang coming in 1986, they thought they should be in the investment banking business. And they bought the best – Wedd Durlacher, the stock jobber (a market maker in the old, demarcated City) was the sector leader and de Zoete and Bevan one of the top stockbrokers. They put the two firms together and for a period after Big Bang, the business boomed. There were a few hiccups along the line but overall, Barclays de Zoete Wedd did very, very well. However, there is no question that the amount of capital being put into the investment bank did not make the returns that you would want and expect. There was always hope that it would, and the idea was that you would hire the best people and the profitability would flow. Which is fine as long as the business cycle carries on, but when a business cycle turns, then a highly-leveraged business, as BZW was, becomes very difficult to manage and justify.

And all along there is the fundamental difference between clearing banking and investment banking. The issue for a clearing bank which buys partnerships, as the two City firms were, was always going to be the vast differential in pay and conditions between the core business and the new investment bank. That was just about kept under control, but it was always lurking. Mixing the two corporate cultures was very, very difficult, the remuneration contrast could lead to basic jealousies, and so on.

Much later in my stint at Barclays, I came to believe that these types of City businesses should never be part of big corporations – effectively, they become workers' cooperatives. All the risk stayed with the bank while all the rewards went to the employees. So Martin Taylor had a strong case for selling BZW. My fundamental criticism of him was that he just didn't make any effort to bring along the NEDs.

This had nothing to do with my personal feelings – it was entirely about good governance. You cannot, as a chief executive, just ignore the NEDs – and if you feel that the NEDs don't understand the business and your cause is hopeless, you should leave the company. By the way, the same goes for the chairman if he or she can't command the support of the board. So I wasn't opposed to Martin over a matter of strategy – it was in all respects about his execution.

The sale of the business was conducted by Goldman Sachs, and they completely misjudged the reaction of the BZW staff in being asked to share their work in progress data with a rival. As a result, the business couldn't be properly valued and was sold to Credit Suisse First Boston (CSFB) for about £100 million, a fraction of what it was worth. To me, the outcome also demonstrated Martin's shortcomings, both in not sharing with the board his views, which were quite legitimate and actually, in hindsight, had merit, and in his lack of commercial nous: he had assumed that it would be easy to get a good price for the business. It is true that BZW's value was impacted by a slump in Asian markets and the resistance of its senior people to an open auction. But the final reality was that the sale process – and the proceeds – were a disaster.

Bill Harrison resigned on principle and took his buccaneering M&A skills elsewhere. Like David Band, he died terribly early, at the age of 57. Taylor then appointed Bob Diamond to head what was seen by the City as BZW's rump, the fixed income and capital markets business, which was rebranded Barclays Capital (BarCap). The board was later joined by Sir Andrew Large, who had been chairman of the Securities and Investment Board, forerunner of the Financial Services Authority (FSA). He became deputy chairman and made no secret to the NEDs of the fact that he wanted to be chairman.

Nigel Mobbs was, to me, the best NED until his retirement in 2003 (he died in 2005). He had been there a long time and taught me an awful lot about the best way to behave and to ask the right questions. He was chairman of the audit committee and he clearly understood, as much as a layman can, the dynamics of the bank.

Oliver Stocken, the finance director who had come from BZW, was very solid and coming up to retirement. Dame Hilary Cropper, who joined a couple of years after me, was good.

Sir Peter Middleton was deputy chairman of the group and chairman of BZW when I joined, and became chairman of Barclays Capital after the disposal. Peter was a former permanent secretary of the Treasury and I liked him enormously. As a former civil servant, he clearly enjoyed the trappings and salary associated with a top bank. He was extremely talented and, as you'd expect, very astute politically.

The tension between many of the NEDs and Martin Taylor came to a head in early October 1998. We had a board meeting coming up in New York, and before we flew over there, I had a meeting with Andrew Buxton, who told me that Martin wanted to split the group, essentially turning Barclays into a retail and small business bank together with Barclaycard, while selling the Barclays Capital investment banking arm or hiving it off as a separate company.

I said: "That's fine, but presumably we are going to receive some papers on this?" And Andrew said that because Martin didn't trust any of the NEDs not to leak this, there were no papers. So I asked if the plan had been discussed at the executive committee. And Andrew didn't seem to know, which appeared odd to me. I had the impression that Andrew and Martin didn't really speak to each other much.

So we flew to New York, and suddenly we were all getting calls in our hotel rooms from journalists because they had got wind of something happening. The board meeting started and we went through the routine part of the business. Then Martin opened up and said that he felt we should split the bank in the way that I had been told by Andrew. But there were no details at all – nothing about how Barclays Capital would be valued, how the two balance sheets would be structured, debt allocation and so on.

Andrew had decided that he would go round the room and ask each NED's views, but first he wanted to know what the executive directors thought. And it rapidly became apparent to me that

Martin had not shared any of this with his executive committee, which was a shock. Then, one by one, the executives on the board said either that they disagreed with the plan or that they did not feel in any position to make a judgment – because no numbers or anything about the consequences of the restructuring had been put forward. The one exception was John Varley, who at the time was head of retail banking services. I like John enormously, but his judgment of people wasn't always the best. He tended to trust, and therefore be very loyal to people, which is a good attribute in most situations but not all. I think he felt that he owed Martin a duty of loyalty, and he was the only director who agreed that the split should be pursued.

I don't know why, but Martin took great exception to the fact that this discussion took place. He put his head in his hands and said that he couldn't go on like this. The whole situation was disturbing, particularly coming after the way the BZW decision had been handled.

Again, the central issue I had was not whether the bank should be split up, which I thought was a perfectly legitimate question for the board to debate on the chief executive's recommendation; my issue was with the lack of corporate governance reflected in the absence of any detailed rationale or information, which I found quite unacceptable. And I was swayed by the fact that the majority of executives thought it was a bad idea. It was not that I believed if you could do the split cleanly the plan would not work; but it was a big 'if'. Splitting the balance sheet of a bank is an incredibly difficult thing to do for regulatory, and a host of other, reasons. And none of this had been thought through by the executive. I had expected a full, detailed plan to be put before the board.

I was not the only NED who felt this way. Nigel Mobbs had arranged for the two of us, once the board meeting was over, to go over to New Jersey and play golf at Pine Valley, the course that has been ranked number one in the world. Nigel hired a stretch limousine to get us there, and on the turnpike from New York we discussed what had happened in the board. Nigel thought that it was totally unacceptable – he had been on the board for a decade and said he was not going to be treated like this. I said: "I know I've not been on the board very long, but I just think it is very strange behaviour."

Nigel went on to say that the situation could not be allowed to continue. And it didn't, because a few weeks later, Martin resigned. We asked Peter Middleton to take over as CEO while we started a search for a long-term successor. Peter was a very safe pair of hands, he fundamentally believed in the integrated bank and he had the support of the executive team. That was the end of all the stuff about splitting the bank, which was a nonsense if the executive didn't back it.

Who do I blame for Martin Taylor's problems with the board? Well, Martin himself has to take quite a lot of responsibility because of his attitude to the NEDs. He was absolutely right that NEDs who aren't bankers cannot know the detail of a bank balance sheet. I'm not sure that, even after 13 years on the board of Barclays, I completely understood how a bank works. What Martin Taylor didn't get is that NEDs with a lot of experience have a feel for people and business, so as a chief executive you have to aim off a little to allow for their lack of knowledge. But you ought to listen to them because their experience means they can sense things, they have a feel for issues. And then everything is a balance. As a CEO or an executive chairman, which I was at Williams throughout its existence, you can ignore the view of a NED or take it on board – but you should at least listen. Martin showed no inclination to listen to anybody at all.

However, I also think Andrew Buxton was culpable, because I have never come across such a dysfunctional board and ultimately, that is down to the chairman. A chairman has very little to do, but one of the crucial things he has to do is make sure that the chief executive carries out a strategy which has been agreed by the board and keeps the board informed. If that CEO refuses to engage with the NEDs or ignores them, he or she has to be counselled by the chairman that they need to change their behaviour. I personally think Martin Taylor was ill-equipped to be a CEO. Nobody could ever doubt his intellect or his integrity, but I did doubt his ability to lead, which came to a head over his plan to split the bank. But if he had had a stronger chairman to guide him and talk to him, it all might have worked. The whole unhappy period strongly shaped my view of the chairman's role, so I suppose you could say that I learned from it. But it was a pretty painful education.

11

Barclays and ABN

Barclays established a board committee, including me, to find a new chief executive and we interviewed a number of external candidates from a list compiled by David Kimbell.

We eventually alighted on a really good candidate, Michael O'Neill, who was chief financial officer of Bank of America. He readily accepted our offer and we announced his appointment in February 1999. Then things got surreal. The week before he was due to start, he called Peter Middleton to say that he was ill and would have to postpone his arrival. Then he postponed again, and finally he said that he was too ill and could not take up the job. We asked him to fly over anyway and got him to a Harley Street specialist where he was diagnosed with arrhythmia. He confirmed that he was unwilling to continue, so the following day, 12 April, we had to announce his withdrawal. Happily, he eventually recovered and went on to become chairman of Citigroup.

We started over and, from Kimbell's second short list, one candidate stood out: Peter (later Sir Peter) Burt, who was chief executive of Bank of Scotland. Even better, we were told that he was really interested in the job. Then something odd happened again.

I was at a function in London and Sir Bob Reid, the former Shell CEO and chairman of British Rail, came up to me. He was now a director of Bank of Scotland and he said: "I'm glad that talks are going well." Of course I didn't know what he was talking about, but I thought to myself, *I'm not going to learn anything if I close this down*, so I replied: "Yes, I think they are."

He then said: "I think the two banks will make a great deal, and Peter is reporting to us that he would be the chief executive of the combined group." I was flabbergasted, but I muttered something about it all being very interesting and moved off.

When I reported this conversation to the committee, we decided that I should quickly arrange to interview Peter Burt to find out what he was really after. Two days later, I met him at Spencer Stuart's office near Hyde Park, and it quickly became very apparent that he had no interest whatsoever in becoming Barclays' chief executive – because he was trying to get into a position where he could merge the two banks. He had told his board one thing while, through the head-hunter, he was purporting to be a candidate for the Barclays position. I've been involved in many searches and they are not generally sources of amusement, but I found this situation hilarious.

Needless to say, when I reported back to the committee, we immediately dropped Peter Burt from the list of candidates. Of course, Burt continued to pursue his dream of bank mega-mergers. First he tried to take over National Westminster (NatWest) but was outbid by Royal Bank of Scotland. Then he merged Bank of Scotland with the Halifax to form HBOS, and finally – during the 2008/9 financial crisis – HBOS got into such trouble that it was gobbled up by Lloyds.

So on we went and, happily, made it third time lucky. We identified Matt Barrett, an Irish–Canadian who was chairman and CEO of Bank of Montreal. I interviewed Matt, whom I found completely engaging and highly amusing. In a sense, he was my kind of person because he had started at the bottom as a Bank of Montreal clerk – no university education – but was clearly astute, possessed several decades of banking experience and had clearly learned volumes from it. We were very aware that he had a colourful personal life, but our focus was on his excellent professional attributes: we thought he would make a big difference to Barclays, and we were proven correct.

Matt became CEO in July 1999 and Peter Middleton moved up to become chairman, which suited him down to the ground. One of the things I noted about Matt was that he was probably the most laid-back executive I've ever come across. I remember a particular board meeting when he was due to give his monthly chief executive's report. Now, you don't expect the CEO to write his entire report – many get someone else to draft it – but generally speaking, you do expect him to have read it and know what's in it. I used to really enjoy the questioning of Matt on his reports because he often hadn't a clue what had been written.

Over and above all that, Matt Barrett was a brilliant intuitive banker. He had some tremendous observations about the nature of the business – for instance, he said that in retail banking, we made no money at all out of operating bank accounts but we made a fortune out of "parking fines" and (in those days) payment protection. Parking fines were overdraft charges. He used to reckon that 200% of our profits came from these two sources. That kind of observation was typical of Matt. He knew what was important and he understood the vulnerability of the retail bank.

The other thing I always remember is what he said about balance sheets. He was very, very aware that across the world, banks were blowing up their balance sheets in their pursuit of growth. One night over dinner, he said to me: "The problem is that both sides of the balance sheet are too big." In other words, it wasn't just the debt side – the leverage – it was also the inflated scale of the assets because the return on them, the margin, was so slim. This insight – in light of what happened later, you could also call it foresight – came from his own experience with the Bank of Montreal in South America. One of the banks they were involved with there had gone bust in an economic downturn, because it was making very tight margins and therefore even a small run on the bank had had catastrophic effects. I actually think that Matt had a foreboding about the financial crisis – he sensed what was going to happen. When he did finally retire from Barclays, he sold all his shares within days.

You would never have called him a typical banker. He was a very charming individual who liked to get out and about after work and who certainly enjoyed female company. In fact, the thing that most worried the board was that he might feature in some paparazzi-related incident outside a night club or whatever. Fortunately most of his coverage stayed in the financial media, where he had a bit of a playboy image. But that belied the wealth of expertise that he brought to the business.

Matt didn't want to be CEO for too long, and after about four years it was apparent that he would want to step down soon. At the same time, Peter Middleton was coming up for five years in the chair which, considering his previous stints as deputy chairman, meant that he was due to retire.

We obviously didn't want to have a completely new chairman and a new CEO at the same time – all companies try to avoid that. At this point, I was asked by John Varley and Bob Diamond to put my name forward to be chairman. This approach was more than flattering. I had certainly learned an awful lot about banking during my eight years on the board. But I firmly believed that the chairman of a bank ought to be a banker. I was neither an investment nor a clearing banker. So I just didn't have the toolkit. And it was clear to me that Matt Barrett did.

The board agreed with me about Matt, and they asked me to broach with Peter the idea that he should think about retiring. This was tricky, because Peter revelled in the chairman's position and was therefore rather cross with me. I found the whole thing quite painful, because I really liked Peter and knew that he had done a huge amount for Barclays. But I felt that I had to carry the message from the board, along with the news that we wanted to replace him with Matt Barrett and that therefore he should start a process of choosing Matt's successor as chief executive. It was eventually agreed that Peter would step down in 18 months' time.

The CEO search became a hugely drawn-out affair, but in the end there were five serious internal candidates – John Varley, Bob

Diamond, Roger Davis (head of the business bank), Gary Hoffman (who ran Barclaycard) and David Roberts (head of retail). However, it was very clear from very early on that Varley was going to be the CEO. It took ages to bring the whole process to a close, but finally John was appointed and Matt Barrett succeeded Peter as chairman. The board appointed me deputy chairman.

Our results under the new leadership were good, but in 2006 it became apparent that Matt Barrett really wanted to retire and we had to find a new chairman. Before the search started, I was asked again whether I would take it on – a delegation of executives came to me and said, "Look Nigel, you have to do it." I was tempted, because being chairman of a bank with the scale of Barclays would have been a really interesting position. But despite all the time I had spent on the board and everything I had learned, I still felt that you need a banker as chairman. As a non-banker, I didn't have sufficient understanding of the business or enough knowledge to control the likes of Bob Diamond and John Varley. And I would have had to give up all sorts of other things I was doing, because despite the fact it was non-executive, I judged it to be a full-time job. So again I said no, and my prize for that was being asked to lead the search for a new chairman.

We searched very hard, looked at a number of Americans, one or two Brits and at the end of the day, my choice was Richard Broadbent, who had joined the board in 2003. I think he would have made an excellent chairman and one of my great regrets is that I didn't push this harder. Bob Diamond in particular was against the appointment, and in retrospect I think he knew that Richard Broadbent was somebody who would be very, very strong. Richard came from the Treasury, had moved into the private sector to a senior role with Schroders, and then run HM Customs and Excise. He was a very accomplished operator. But I reluctantly backed down and I think that was a huge mistake, both by the board as a whole and by me.

We then went for Marcus Agius, chairman of Lazards, who was a very well-connected investment banker. I put it to the board that Marcus was not an aggressive character, but I had worked out that, if we appointed him, he would effectively be president of the bank, John Varley would be executive chairman and Bob Diamond the CEO. I thought that this would work. John sub-let just about all the day-to-day running to Bob. Marcus would make a very good job of what might appear to be a rather superficial, figure-head role: he would do all the dinners, he would interact with people; he was very good at opening things and making speeches.

In fact, Marcus had a very important role in the management balance that we had at the top of the bank. He also looked the part. Have you ever seen anyone as immaculately dressed and impeccably mannered as Marcus? Somebody joked that the only way you could make him angry was to go up and straighten his tie! His wife Kate was a Rothschild, so he had married into banking royalty. Anyway, I decided that Marcus Agius was the man. The board agreed. And everything went fine for the bank until the financial crisis.

Our strategy now was to become one of the world's leading universal banks. Barclays had always believed that banks needed to be bigger – certainly that European banks had to expand to match the scale of the leading Americans. We toyed with the idea of approaching the UK government to see if we could merge with Lloyds. But this was obviously going to be a very difficult proposition and would fall foul of all sorts of competition issues. We also considered American banks – we looked at Lehman for years, we looked at Wachovia, I think we even looked at Wells Fargo. We felt that we should be multinational – we didn't think that just being a British-based bank would cut it.

The only large bank in Europe that seemed to be badly-managed and undervalued was ABN Amro in the Netherlands. It had under-performed for years but, with its Dutch connections, had a very good franchise in the Far East. It would also give us a really good position in mainland Europe. We were considering making a move when, in early 2007, their chairman Rijkman Groenink approached

John Varley about a deal and talks then took place over a number of months. I was on the transaction committee that we set up, so I got all the details of what was being negotiated. An awful lot of our time was spent on what are commonly called domestic or social issues – in other words, the five principles that the Duport guy had counted off on the fingers of one hand when Williams was buying them: "What's In It For Me?"

We eventually persuaded them to do a deal. We knew that a cash bid was out of the question because our ratios would be totally out of sync. So this was predominantly a shares deal, valuing ABN at about £67 billion. We were aware that we might face competition – we had intelligence that Royal Bank of Scotland (RBS) had been looking at ABN as well. Their CEO Fred Goodwin was paranoid about Barclays being bigger than the Royal Bank. Anyway, we launched the offer and RBS then formed a consortium which bid slightly higher and almost entirely in cash.

And then the financial markets started to crash.

We first registered what was happening in early August, when the German bank West LB suspended some investor redemptions and then BNP Paribas of France froze three of its derivatives funds. I remember a board meeting where Chris Lucas, our finance director, reported that short-term money markets were becoming very, very difficult: money was drying up and what there was of it was becoming increasingly expensive. We had some discussion about reducing our exposures and so on, but there was always a fear that we would be criticised in the market for surrendering share. Which is a crazy thing in a bank, of course. Nevertheless, that was the business climate at the time.

Then came the collapse of Northern Rock. Barclays had a close-up view of what had been going on in the UK mortgage market, because when Matt Barrett was CEO we had bought the Woolwich, one of the leading British building societies. We paid £5.4 billion for it but over the ensuing years just about all that value disappeared as we lost market share to Northern Rock and HBOS. We really couldn't understand the economics of their pricing and we determined not to follow them. Which at the end of the day was not a bad thing. One area where Barclays did not get caught by the crash was the UK mortgage market, because in effect they had written off the whole value of the Woolwich.

We did get hit in the US mortgage market, which we had belatedly entered in 2006 through the acquisition of a company called EquiFirst. By contrast with some, our outlay was quite small – we only paid $76 million for EquiFirst whereas HSBC had spent all of $16 billion a few years earlier on Household International. But there's no question that we went into the US mortgage business because everyone else had. I remember thinking that this was quite strange, because I had seen how slight the margin on mortgages was in the UK. Interest-only mortgages, cashbacks – they were all going on. When you stood back from it, you couldn't understand how anyone could make money. The only way was to leverage up 50 or 60 times. Crazy.

We knew who the US business was lending to – the so-called sub-prime borrowers. And that the banks were then ranking the mortgages from low-risk to high-risk, parcelling them up into assorted packages and then selling each package on to insurance companies or whoever. So I was under the impression that we weren't holding this stuff on the balance sheet. Now that was extremely naïve and maybe I should have asked the question, but I just assumed that we were in the business of wholesaling these sub-prime mortgages. When the short-term money markets tightened up, these things became unsaleable and it became apparent that, in fact, we did have quite a lot on the balance sheet.

The explosion of leverage went far beyond the mortgage market. Big corporate transactions designed to boost companies' market share were being done on a covenant-lite or no-covenant basis. As chairman of Boots, I saw the other side of this: after the KKR offer was agreed, Bob Diamond rang me up and asked me to get Barclays on the list of lenders that KKR was lining up for its huge debt issue – £10 billion or whatever it was. I think Barclays took £1 billion of that and within weeks, it was trading at half the value.

Stefano Pessina and KKR made a fortune buying that discounted debt back in – they probably made more doing that than from the actual Boots transaction.

At the same time, during late 2007 and early 2008, Barclays was continuing to dash for growth in international retail banking. John Varley had appointed a guy called Frits Seegers from Citigroup to run retail, and he expanded all over the place: Spain, Portugal, Italy, Uganda, the Middle East, Russia, Indonesia, Pakistan, India. I remember sitting next to Richard Broadbent in a board meeting where Frits proudly announced that they had signed something like 60,000 new customers in India just that past week. We just looked at each other in amazement.

When the crash came, this indiscriminate growth cost Barclays billions in write-offs – I was told £5 billion or £6 billion was the total. Eventually, John Varley had to get rid of Seegers. John is a lovely man, extremely erudite, but he wasn't all that streetwise and he didn't like confrontation. Sometimes, confrontation is inevitable.

Seegers wasn't the only one who seemed oblivious of the worsening money markets. At one point before Northern Rock blew up, I met a non-executive director of HBOS and asked him if he realised the obvious risks they were running in effectively buying UK mortgage market share, and he didn't seem that concerned. I've since spoken to Andy Hornby (HBOS's former CEO), and he said that he was very nervous about the strategy of maintaining market share against the likes of Northern Rock, but that they were under so much pressure to follow that line – they were being castigated by analysts and investors for losing share.

I sympathised with him, because everyone is always smart after the event, but when you are running a company, you are driven in many ways by the City and by market expectations. We've all been in those situations, and as a board you have to be very, very strong if you believe that your strategy, however unpopular, is right. You must have the courage of your convictions, and the beauty of having a strong chairman is that he or she can give air cover to the CEO. That's what Richard Baker and I did at Boots – we were hated by the City for cutting our prices and issuing profit warnings, but it was the right thing to do for the business in the longer term. If ever you start being driven by analysts and the City into what they think you should be doing to bolster the share price in the short term, or to get short-term plaudits, then it can quite often lead to disaster. You should always do what you think is right.

Incidentally, when Northern Rock collapsed, all the papers said there hadn't been a run on a bank in the UK since the 1930s, but that was wrong. There was actually one that my mother was involved in – on 4 February 1971, to be precise – the day Rolls-Royce went bankrupt.

Derby was Rolls' home town, then as now, and when the truly shocking news about the bankruptcy broke that day, a rumour started to fly around the streets that the Derbyshire Building Society was heavily invested in Rolls. A queue formed in the centre of Derby, and snaked around the market place, a queue of people trying to take their money out of the Derbyshire Building Society. I was walking by and I spotted my mother in the queue, so I asked her: "What are you doing?" And she told me that "All our savings" (which didn't amount to very much) were in the building society and "I want our money out." Across the square was the Halifax, and there was an almost equally big queue outside it with people wanting to deposit the money they'd just taken from the Derbyshire. They were carrying piles of cash across the road. So Northern Rock wasn't the first bank crash in 75 years – but it was a pretty big moment and it heralded the meltdown that happened a year later, in September 2008.

In this environment, we simply could not believe that RBS was ploughing on with its £70 billion cash bid for ABN while inside Barclays, we were discussing whether we would invoke force majeure so we could pull our offer. It was obvious that RBS's reserves and equity ratios would be shot to pieces by such a bid. And we couldn't understand why the financial regulator, the Financial Services Authority (FSA) was allowing this to happen.

The FSA wasn't the only regulator which, in my opinion, fell down on the job. I had done economics for one term in the sixth form, but I knew well enough that the Bank of England was the lender of last resort. In the case of Northern Rock, whose failure started the financial avalanche, I think the governor of the Bank of England should have stepped in and stood behind the bank. The government would have had to commit guarantees, but it wouldn't have collapsed and everything would have been orderly. Instead, the governor sat on his hands, talking about moral hazard. And the consequences were huge.

My argument about moral hazard is simply that it is theoretical economics. In the real world, banks are inherently unstable and will always push stuff to the limit. It is up to the regulators to stop them. I don't care what kind of leverage you have – if everyone wants their money out of a bank on a particular day, no bank in the world can liquidate such vast sums and stay afloat. It is therefore a nonsense to believe that any kind of bank can withstand a total run. Regulators should have understood that. I think they do now. In fact, we have gone the other way and it has led to over-capitalisation of the banks, which actually retards business.

Anyway, with the regulators standing back, RBS won the bid battle against us for ABN and that's what you could really call a Pyrrhic victory. Their consortium partners, Santander of Spain and the Belgian–Dutch Fortis, took the best bits of ABN and left RBS with the rump. The purchase price made RBS 50 times geared. It was complete madness. But it got Barclays off the hook. Our downside was limited anyway, because ours was a paper offer; in fact, our ratios would in theory have improved. But the write-offs we would have had to make would have been pretty severe, so on balance I think it would have been a disastrous deal for us – but not nearly so disastrous as the cash deal was for Royal Bank of Scotland. They saved Barclays.

Receiving the Institute of Chartered Accountants' Founding Societies' Award

12

Barclays and Lehman

The first half of 2008 was something of a phoney war in terms of the financial crisis, because conditions in the markets were obviously bad but the roof hadn't yet fallen in.

In July, we had a board meeting where Bob Diamond presented what was called Project Long Island – a bid to buy Lehman Brothers, which was obviously in trouble. The attraction of Lehman was that it would catapult Barclays into the universal banking elite because it was a big player in the US equity and bond markets where Barclays had little or no presence because of the sale of BZW. The downside was that it was obviously going to be a very difficult deal to pull off, particularly because no-one, including the US government, could tell exactly how bad a state Lehman was in. It had amassed huge investments in sub-prime assets, whose value had collapsed.

Lehman's situation got much worse and in early September we had a flurry of board meetings to discuss Barclays' interest. By now, Bob Diamond was over in the US talking to the head of the Fed – the US Federal Reserve – and everybody else about acquiring it. I said very early on in the board's conversation that our bid, which was worth $3.8 billion, would not work because its size meant that it would be a Class 1 transaction – in other words that it would require shareholder approval at an extraordinary general meeting. You cannot agree to buy a bank in trouble on the basis that shareholders would have the right to reject the bid three weeks later. The interregnum would be impossible to bridge.

It wasn't just about the unquantifiable liabilities – in fact, the US government and the Fed were putting together a package deal with the other Wall Street banks to take a lot of the toxic stuff and create a kind of bad bank – it was the lack of time available: in that timescale, to do the requisite due diligence and everything else, it was going to be almost impossible.

Nobody seemed to take much notice of me and the negotiations continued, culminating over the weekend of 13–14 September when we had three or four board meetings. After each meeting I still had absolutely no sense that the deal would ever be done. People were running around like mad and I kept on saying, "It isn't going to happen." As far as the US government was concerned, Bank of America had been planning to take over Lehman, but at the last minute it decided to buy Merrill Lynch, leaving Barclays as the sole bidder for Lehman. Finally, on the Sunday afternoon, Hank Paulson – a former head of Goldman Sachs who had been appointed US treasury secretary – called his UK counterpart, chancellor of the exchequer Alistair Darling, to ask if the British government would allow Barclays to buy Lehman and waive the rights of the Barclays shareholders to have an EGM.

Darling, who I actually think was the best player in the crisis by a long way, told Paulson that the government would not support a Barclays bid, on the grounds that (a), he didn't have the power to override the EGM and (b), that it was going to be extremely risky for Barclays and the UK financial regulators were therefore not prepared to back it. From that moment, the deal was dead. We all went back to what we had been doing before the weekend, and Lehman duly went bust. When the news broke on Monday morning, 15 September, confidence in the banking system was up-ended, financial markets slumped and the storm that had been brewing for months finally broke.

To Bob Diamond's credit, he had spotted an opportunity in the Lehman wreckage, which was the chance to snap up the bit that we really wanted, the US equities and corporate finance business. Over that week and with lots of board meetings, we agreed to pay $1.75 billion for this business. This was a great deal, financially and strategically – the head office freehold alone was worth about as much as the total purchase price – because Bob is a very bright guy. He's a super salesman really. And he had the ability, a bit like Brian Clough in a way, to get the most out of people. He paid them huge sums of money, but he also got tremendous loyalty from them.

Even looked at today, taking into account the crisis and its consequences, Lehman US was an extremely advantageous deal for Barclays because it took all the best assets and the goodwill but none of Lehman's toxic liabilities. In any other circumstances, it would have been the absolute making of Barclays as a world leader. But of course, what nobody grasped at the time, including the US government, was the extent of the crisis that was triggered by allowing Lehman to go under.

In the UK, Lloyds agreed to take over HBOS, which almost brought Lloyds down, while RBS was in terminal trouble. That led in early October to the government's bailout of the banks in which it nationalised both RBS and Lloyds–HBOS. The key question for Barclays was whether we would get pulled into the government lifeboat, which would have meant that the bank would effectively come under state control. The board was unanimously opposed to this and we didn't see the need for it: we had a number of board meetings and we concluded that Barclays could survive without government money, but that we would need some additional financial support which we aimed to find somewhere in the international markets, and we looked at all sorts of options.

There came a critical point in March 2009 where the government wanted Barclays stress-tested by the FSA. If we failed the test, then they could have strong-armed us into their lifeboat. Some quite draconian scenarios were put forward in terms of the economy, to see whether Barclays would have sufficient liquidity to ride out these projections. We eagerly awaited the results of the stress test and on the morning of the day this was due, John Varley called each board member to say that he was going to receive the results at around lunchtime from Hector Sants, the FSA's chief executive.

In fact, Varley had two calls from Sants that day – a preliminary one saying Barclays seemed to have passed the tests and then a later confirmation that this was the case. What happened then was bizarre: the first edition of the *Financial Times* came out, falsely reporting that we had failed the stress test. John Varley, to his eternal credit, then asked Hector Sants to email him so that we would have written confirmation that we had passed. And as soon as John received the email, we put out an RNS – a Stock Exchange announcement – saying that we had passed. And the *Financial Times* had to change the story.

There is no question in my mind that someone in the Treasury – and I have a pretty good idea who it was – had rung the *FT* in a bid to destabilise Barclays, because the government wanted Barclays within the ring of government-controlled banks. We never knew precisely why, but we assumed that the prime minister, Gordon Brown, did not want any of the banks to be outside his control – probably for the very legitimate reason that, if Barclays remained independent and went bust six months later, it would prolong the financial crisis. But we will never know.

This, in my opinion, started the vendetta that the government and other regulatory authorities had against Barclays. We were never forgiven for having avoided the state rescue package. We did have to raise capital, and we considered various options including some very strange people from Libya and Russia who were immediately dismissed. But the Qataris were the obvious candidates. We had a relationship with them already and eventually, we did a fund-raising deal with them.

At this point, I spoke to Marcus Agius and said that, if we were to proceed with the Qatari deal, we had let our shareholders partici-pate because we could not deny them pre-emption rights. Marcus said that Barclays had considered this, advised by JP Morgan, and decided that in the timescale involved, this was not possible. I said that ignoring the rights of our existing shareholders would be a disaster with them, and so it turned out to be. At the ensuing annual general meeting, Marcus was castigated and – being the gentleman that he is – he has always acknowledged that I was the one person who said we ought not to treat the shareholders this way.

This was an instance of what a business person with investor relations experience could see: I was not a banker, but I had been around the City and raised money, so I knew that pre-emption is a critical factor with institutions, an absolutely fundamental principle, and that you deny them the right to avoid dilution at your peril. The Qatari deal eventually led to court cases in 2019–20, where I was very pleased to see that the Barclays individuals accused were rightly cleared. But because of the pre-emption rights issue, the deal caused real and long-lasting damage to our relations with the City: I think it's one of the main reasons why Barclays has been disliked over the years by the institutional community.

There were several strange conversations during this period, and the most troubling one I had was with a government minister. I was in South Africa on holiday and was asked to take a call from Whitehall. The minister said that he thought I had raised issues about the valuation of some of Barclays' assets. I told him this was not true – I had done no such thing. He said that he had been told on good authority that I was very unhappy about these valuations, and then he got quite angry with me. He made a comment along the lines that Barclays would not get away with whatever it was that we were supposed to be doing. Which I thought was absolutely outrageous. I have never spoken to him since.

The story about valuation issues resurfaced a bit later, when I stepped down from the Barclays board. The *Daily Mail* ran a story saying I had resigned because I was unhappy with the valuation of Barclays' assets. I will never know where that story came from but nothing could have been further from the truth – I retired from the board because I'd been on it for 14 years and was in my fifth year as deputy chairman, which was enough for me.

Barclays was a target for all sorts of people. My former adviser Roland Rudd, founder of the public relations company Finsbury, was advising Lloyds and its chairman Victor Blank, my old board colleague from Williams. As I knew from his work with me, Roland is a very smart operator. He was always asking me about Barclays and I suspected he might be looking for information to deflect attention from the problems at Lloyds, which were very big after the takeover of HBOS. So I didn't tell him anything.

I think that to this day there is a residual resentment of Barclays in the City. Throughout my board tenure and since, we have always been seen as a bit too clever by half – all that kind of stuff. I never saw that in Barclays – I certainly never felt we were knowingly doing anything that was unethical or that crossed a line.

Barclays Capital is at the centre of all this, because by building that business, Bob Diamond created a profit machine for Barclays which no other UK bank had, but which a lot of them envied. First he did it in the UK and then he compounded its value by buying Lehman.

BarCap is a fascinating case. In the early days after Martin Taylor sold BZW, it was very small. It just had the Treasury remits and stuff. In fact, many people both inside and outside the bank thought it was just a matter of time before Bob moved on. But they had a group, run by Roger Jenkins and Iain Abrahams, called Structured Finance, which was novel at the time and basically specialised in organising quite complex schemes to shelter the corporation tax liabilities of large banks around the world. I asked several times if we were breaking the letter or the spirit of the law, and was assured – and I think this was right – that all these schemes were approved by the authorities. And this business was the cornerstone on which Bob built BarCap. It was hugely profitable – it made £300m or £400m a year.

The flipside of Structured Finance's success was that the bonuses enjoyed by its team were enormous, because their deal was to take a percentage of the unit's profits. I was remuneration committee chairman for a while and used to have great difficulty agreeing to these sums. But I had to agree to them, both because they were contractual and because they were making a huge amount of money for the bank. While it lasted, which it did for a decade before the crisis, Barclays was making a very good return.

The fantastic returns from Structured Finance enabled Bob to start other businesses, to hire more people. There was a project called Project Alpha where we were hiring the very, very best people. It took months for new areas to be successful and the profitability of Structured Finance provided the smokescreen behind which they could be given time to come through. Initially, the fledgling units might lose £100m a year, but since Structured Finance was doing £300m in profit, the whole thing was making £200m. Then all of a sudden, the new businesses would break out. And that's how Barclays got a full-scale capital markets business. It was strategically very clever and Bob did a great job there.

I think the problem with Bob came when John Varley retired. This was after I left the board of course, but I watched the situation closely. As I said, I always looked at the leadership as a triumvirate: Marcus was president, John was effectively executive chairman and Bob was the CEO. That wasn't what their official titles said, but it was the reality and it was a very well-balanced ticket. They complemented each other.

John's departure upset that balance. He had always said that he wanted to retire at the age of 55 and true to his word, he did. I knew instinctively that the board would appoint Bob as chief executive and I always thought that this was a mistake. It wouldn't have been a mistake if Marcus had also been replaced with a stronger chairman. This would have been a big call, because it would have been changing the two top positions at the same time, something companies normally bend over backwards to avoid. Marcus was a highly experienced investment banker but he was not somebody who could totally control Bob and I said that to a number of my former board colleagues after the decision was made. They claimed that they really had no choice because Bob would have left if they hadn't made him CEO. And that was undoubtedly true. But it didn't deal with the other part of the equation, which I told them I would have argued for – OK, make Bob chief executive but we have to bring in a big shot American banker as chairman who will understand and control what Bob was doing.

I've seen it a number of times over the years – problems arising when you have companies with a very forceful CEO and a chairman who isn't strong enough to handle and guide the chief executive. In banking, where it's so important for the chairman to understand the intricacies of the business, the classic case was Royal Bank of Scotland when they appointed Tom McKillop from AstraZeneca as chairman and Fred Goodwin was CEO. McKillop knew a bit about banking because he had been on the board of Lloyds, but he wasn't a banker.

The Libor scandal really hit Barclays hard and matters went from bad to worse. They were hit by a number of mis-steps, the final one being Bob's disastrous appearance before the House of Commons Treasury select committee inquiry into the scandal, which I watched with horror. I think a strong chairman would have told him exactly how to behave: not to act like an American, calling the committee members by their Christian names and doing that kind of soft soap thing. That they are not there to be your friends – rather the opposite, they are trying to trip you up. The whole thing was gruesome.

Still, the committee hearing was a bit of a sideshow after the main event because the Bank of England had effectively forced Bob to resign already. That was disgraceful, but the Bank of England was party to the vendetta against Barclays that dated from the financial crisis. Mervyn King, who was governor of the BOE during the crisis, hated how Barclays had acted – resisting the government bailout and all that – and I think the BOE viewed Bob as the chief culprit. Where they had control over other banks, those that were in the lifeboat, the authorities had been able to force through management changes. But Barclays had stayed beyond their reach and they always resented that. By 2012, when the Libor storm broke, Bob was the last surviving CEO of the three big British banks caught up in the financial crisis (HSBC had sailed through it, relatively speaking). That's why, when Marcus very honourably offered to resign immediately because of Libor and the board accepted his decision, the BOE called him in and said that they wanted Bob gone, not Marcus.

Yet Barclays has maintained its place as Britain's only player in the world banking league. It's a funny thing – Barclays is almost taken for granted in London, it's given no credit – but it's the only one of the British banks that has actually made it internationally as a big universal bank, including in the US. And that's Bob's legacy, and John's, and Marcus's, and that of the others who were there during my years on the board. It was an extraordinary experience. We kept our independence through the biggest financial crisis in 80 years and we took a lot of flak in the process – flak from some very heavy guns. Despite all this, Barclays remains just about the only effective European competitor to the large US banks. It surely deserves some credit for being the last one standing.

13

Invensys

During 2008, the Boots deal was done and dusted and I knew that I would be leaving Barclays before too long, so I had the capacity to take on a new chairmanship. At this point I had a call from Jan Hall, who had founded and built her firm JCA into one of the leading London head-hunters. She asked me if I would be interested in Invensys and my instant and somewhat discouraging reply was, "Well, it's a bit of a mess, isn't it?"

To her credit, Jan did not miss a beat. She said: "Yes it is, and that's why some of the directors want you to be chairman. They aren't happy with the existing chairman. But it's a split board, and the shareholders and the advisers are getting quite worried about the situation."

I never pigeon-holed myself as a chairman-trouble-shooter, but I was a change-agent where change was needed. So I said: "OK, I will look at it."

There was a lot of history to Invensys, which was created by the 1999 merger of two struggling conglomerates, BTR and Siebe. I knew both companies, in fact I had been called several years before the merger by Ian Strachan, then chief executive of BTR, who asked me for some advice on how to handle the fraught situation there.

Like the other conglomerates including Williams, BTR had revelled in the acquisition wave of the 1980s and had done very, very well during inflationary times. Its management was always quick to push up prices and duly reaped the returns. But it had been caught out by the fundamental changes in the market during the 1990s – the changes that also affected Williams – and had ended up with a collection of rather poor businesses in areas that either had run out of growth already or were about to do so. The difference between us was that, at Williams, we recognised that times were changing and we streamlined the group accordingly; BTR didn't. Admittedly, it was much larger than Williams and was therefore harder to manage down, but by the time it saw the writing on the wall, the company as an independent entity with a future was beyond recall.

BTR was basically left with one quality business, Westinghouse Brake & Signal, which was still a contender in the global rail industry, albeit in a niche area. In light of future events, a little more history is relevant here. Westinghouse had originally been part of Hawker Siddeley, the electrical engineering group celebrated for its aerospace business (which made aircraft wings). Hawker's chairman, Sir Arnold Hall, had the foresight to join the Franco-German Airbus consortium in 1969, after the British government had pulled out. As a result, Britain (through Hawker) got a 20% stake in Airbus. But those were Hawker's glory days. In 1977, Labour nationalised the aerospace business and through the 1980s the sprawling group fell on increasingly hard times.

In 1991, Hawker tried to refocus by divesting a bunch of businesses including rail. It was in the final stages of selling Westinghouse to Germany's Siemens when BTR made a hostile bid for the whole of Hawker. Siemens was scared off and BTR won the takeover battle. It was actually BTR's last big acquisition and a Pyrrhic victory – most of Hawker's businesses were struggling and, once inside BTR, they only compounded the decline that ultimately led to the Siebe merger and Invensys.

Siebe was also on the slide, although many people did not realise that. It was a strange company – it was founded in the early nineteenth century by a former Austrian cavalry officer and had made the world's first diving suit. At the turn of the 1980s, it was reinvented by Barrie Stephens – who kept one of those original diving suits in his head office in Windsor – through a series of acquisitions, most of which weren't up to much. There was one exception: Foxboro in the US, which had developed a market-leading automation business for controlling the production processes in big plants like oil refineries and chemical works.

I am sure that Foxboro was a great deal at the time. No-one in the UK had ever heard of it when Stephens came out of nowhere and bought it. A deal like that can keep a company running for years, and it made Siebe a fortune. But even great deals don't stay that way forever. The trouble came when Foxboro's technology was challenged by new systems and the profits began to ebb away. Siebe's accounts did not reveal the extent of the decline. I remember looking at them in the Williams days and found some strange things there: they capitalised a lot of items, including something that was called 'own work' – I think basically it was all the software development, the cost of the engineers, everything. You could certainly call it creative, but the City in general had not recognised the real state of the company at the time of the BTR merger, which was actually a takeover by Siebe. Immediately after the deal the group, which was renamed Invensys for some strange reason, had a market value of about £6 billion – a big discount to annual sales of £9 billion but enough to put it well into the FTSE 100.

The chickens came home to roost with a vengeance in the early 2000s. Stephens had been succeeded by Allen Yurko, who was a protégé of the guys who had run Tyco and who tried to prop up the business by buying a bunch of indifferent companies or worse – he ended up paying more than a billion pounds for Baan, which was a loss-making Dutch software business trying to compete with SAP. I kept an eye on Invensys and had to laugh when I heard that Yurko had described Baan as "a profit waiting to happen." It all ended in a complete mess, Invensys almost collapsed under a mountain of debt and Yurko duly departed and returned to his native America.

Yurko was succeeded as CEO by Rick Haythornthwaite, who had made his name in the City by selling the Blue Circle cement company to the French for a big price. He hired a turnround specialist called Ulf Henriksson from Honeywell. They carried out a huge restructuring, which brought the debt down to manageable but still high levels. Haythornthwaite left after the restructuring and Ulf became CEO. He was highly thought of in the City due to all the work he had done in improving, closing or selling businesses. His restructuring saved Invensys but many problems remained. It was basically a basket case. When I asked a friend of mine who knew the business, he just said: "When you mix *merde* with *merde*, you just get a bigger pile of *merde*."

The chairman was Martin Jay, who had been at GEC under Arnold Weinstock and later became CEO and then chairman of the shipbuilder, VT Group. By now, the board was very nervous and unstable. Jay wanted to stay another three years and there were people who supported him, but another group wanted him to go.

Eventually, the majority of the board insisted that they wanted a change of chairman, so I said that I would join the board for two or three months and see how things worked out. I would take over as chairman if I felt that I could make a difference, and if I wasn't nervous about the business. Martin Jay resented me even being in the office – I could sense the animosity. He knew that I was being lined up as his successor and he didn't want to go. I remember that in one board meeting, we had been talking for two or three hours but he refused to have a comfort break, so I just walked out.

However, I initially had some good conversations with Ulf, who had a terrible relationship with Jay; they hardly spoke and there was no respect from either side. Ulf would propose restructuring ideas, and Martin Jay would resist them. Ulf also thought he deserved to be paid more and all in all, there was a complete clash of cultures as well as personalities – Jay's traditional British background versus Ulf's Americanisation. Board meetings were interminable – they meandered around and were truly awful. Ulf used a kind of management speak that nobody really understood, and I noticed at the time that he was continually talking about reorganisation, even of businesses that seemed stable. Change was his thing, but it should have sounded a warning bell for me.

Anyway, I decided I would accept the invitation to become chairman, and Martin Jay reluctantly retired. I then went to meet the senior people in the company and to visit a number of the businesses. One of my first points of introduction was at a management conference in Palm Beach, Florida. This was an early opportunity for me to see and hear from the Invensys executives, but the insight I actually gained was rather different from what I had expected.

Ulf relied quite heavily on a management guru who made a big presentation at the conference. And to be frank, for the first time in my life, this presentation was something that I just didn't understand at all. What he was saying to these people was almost mystical, and certainly surreal. My immediate thought was, *this guy is taking large sums of money out of the company in fees*. He obviously saw me looking rather askance, and came up to me afterwards and said: "You don't get this, do you?" And I said: "I don't get this at all. I have run businesses for the last 30 years and, quite frankly, I don't know what you are talking about."

Ulf took exception to this and we had a bit of a row. And at that point, I started to realise that Ulf was somebody I could not deal with long-term. He carried on saying, as he had with Martin Jay, that he was relatively underpaid – numerous meetings I had with him were either on the subject of remuneration or degenerated into talk about it. We benchmarked this and found that, in fact, he was quite well paid. But the company was struggling to make much progress, so the situation was very difficult.

For me, the critical moment arrived when Ulf embarked on another huge reorganisation which, far from being helpful, was actually unsettling for the company and the people in it. At this point, I spoke to the board and said, I think this strategy is destabilising and could even be dangerous.

Invensys was fundamentally unstable, so the last thing it needed was even more uncertainty. After all the years of upheaval – the post-merger crisis, the multiple disposals, the debt reduction and operational reorganisation – it was basically a pension fund with a company attached. It was not one of those companies with a big pension net deficit, but in aggregate its gross liabilities were huge relative to its market value. This was the legacy of the disastrous Siebe–BTR deal and it was a dead weight on the company. In that sense, Invensys was like Pilkington, which never recovered financially from the Revlon acquisition. It couldn't break free from the mistakes of its past: the legacy had cost it too much time and money to be able to recapture the ground it had lost to its competitors.

In terms of the actual businesses left after all the restructuring, two – rail and operations management (the software process automation business) – were major and there was a smaller hardware division which supplied heating and air conditioning controls. Rail was well run by James Drummond, whom I knew from Kidde where he had worked in strategy and business development, and who went on to become a CEO in his own right. But it was one of the very few signalling businesses in the industry which either wasn't part of, or didn't have an alliance with, a locomotive manufacturer. So it couldn't provide an integrated offer and was always going in with other manufacturers on major contracts.

Nevertheless, it had some valuable market positions. We had a very big share in the UK on both the overground network and the London Underground, and we had started to bid for contracts around the world. Much of Europe was a closed shop because Germany's Siemens and France's Alstom dominated those markets, so we had to grow elsewhere. We had a very nice business in Spain which was highly profitable and extremely well run, but further afield in Asia and Latin America we had some problems: there was a loss-making contract in Singapore, in Caracas they weren't really paying us and Sao Paulo wasn't very lucrative either.

I soon reached the conclusion that Ulf should leave, but before obtaining the board's approval to remove him I decided to talk to our finance director, Wayne Edmunds, who was impressive and whom I had got to like. Wayne was more than a CFO, because he had previously been strategy director for operations management.

He was one of the people in Invensys I could rely on, but he was clearly finding it very difficult to have any kind of relationship with Ulf and I thought we were in great danger of losing him.

I invited Wayne into my office and said simply: "If Ulf were to leave, would you take over as chief executive?" I added that it was likely to be a short-term assignment because the business would have to be sold or something would have to be done about the pension fund. It was not a stable situation. Wayne understood this and said that he would become CEO if I asked him to do the job. I then went to the board, where there was unanimity on the course of action that we needed to pursue. The other non-executives had got a sense of Wayne's capabilities from his presence at board meetings, and agreed with me. I would ask Ulf to step down and Wayne would become CEO. I had learned from my experience at Williams: I insisted that, before I spoke to Ulf, each non-executive director sign a letter agreeing to the planned change. I was not going to be undermined at the last minute again.

I then made an appointment to see Ulf for breakfast on the following Monday morning at the Goring Hotel, a boutique hotel near Buckingham Palace which was close to the Invensys head office. Martin Reed, a fellow NED who ran the software group Logica, offered to come with me, which I thought was pretty good of him.

I had organised a private room, on the ground floor for ease of arrival and departure, and made sure I arrived before Ulf. When he came in, I invited him to sit down. Before we started eating, I told him that the board wished him to resign, with immediate effect. And he replied that I wouldn't have the support of the other directors. I then showed him the letter with all the board signatures – the 'death warrant'.

Ulf was visibly shocked and very quiet. I told him his best bet was to go into private equity, which was always looking for top-notch turnround experts, and actually I think he has made quite a bit of money doing that.

We parted, and the company then made the announcement to the City. The reaction, as I had anticipated, was one of anger. A number of senior fund managers including Richard Buxton, then at Schroders, rang me up and variously said I was a vandal, someone who didn't realise that Ulf was a hugely successful chief executive, and that I clearly didn't know what I was doing.

I took all this – which, as I said, did not surprise me – and when each one had finished, I arranged to see them over the next week or two. At these meetings, I explained to them that a high-profile chief executive who is liked by the City is not always acting in the best interests of the company as judged by the board. The directors are best placed to know whether this is the case. As has been proved many times, shareholders may own the company but they don't always know what is going on inside it. And for the most part, quite rightly, there are board responsibilities of confidentiality and these things don't get out.

By now, I had accumulated a lot of experience in dealing with and assessing chief executives, and I was absolutely convinced that I had done the right thing. The City reaction was totally predictable: they thought Ulf was a superman and that Nigel Rudd coming along and firing him was just a clash of personalities – two big guys who couldn't get on. That I had fired him for no particular reason other than I wanted my own person in. Nothing could be further from the truth. For a start, I have never changed a chief executive because I personally didn't like him. I have changed him if and when I felt that someone new could do more for the business at that point. As someone said in a different context, it's never personal – it's strictly business.

In Ulf's case, it became clear to me that he was unsuited to sorting out Invensys given the state it had reached and what it had been through. What it needed above all at that point was as much stability – including line management stability – as it could get. I've no doubt that Ulf had done an excellent job in preventing a collapse when that was a real possibility. That was his forte – he was a crisis manager who believed in constant revolution. But when I got there, I found a very uncertain environment where people in the company did not always know either where they were going to be working or who they were going to be reporting to from one day to the next. As a result, morale was awful. But of course, nobody outside saw that.

This is the kind of issue that can and does arise when you have a chief executive with a particular skill set who is lauded by investors for his past success. The time can come, as it did with Invensys, when a very different skill set is needed. But the CEO who is brilliant at crisis management may come to believe his or her own publicity and think that they walk on water. You can even get situations where they may start to ignore the board because they consider themselves bigger than the company. That didn't happen at Invensys, but I have seen it occur in some companies. And the problem for a board of directors is having the guts to call it out. That's where the chairman comes in, because he or she has to take a lead.

Even the best CEOs can stay too long, and boards are very reluctant to take on a powerful and, to that date, successful CEO. Terry Leahy is a case in point. He is a quality operator who was fantastically successful at Tesco, but in my opinion he stayed too long there. Since leaving Tesco, he has been hugely successful in guiding companies such as B&M Stores. I just think that seven or eight years at the top of an organisation is enough for both the individual and the company.

If the board, led by the chairman, does take action to change a CEO, it then has another challenge, which is to decide on the right successor. When I am leading the appointment of a chief executive, I take it very, very seriously. That may sound like a superfluous remark, but I think that sometimes boards facing such a crucial decision don't do all the work that they should. They don't examine all the issues, such as whether there is a cultural fit, or whatever.

In some cases it becomes very obvious that this kind of mistake has been made – that's when the new CEO has to be replaced after a matter of months. But there are plenty of other instances where a board decides to struggle on, even if the non-executives realise they have chosen the wrong person. I've come on to boards in precisely that situation. You have to build up as complete a picture as you can, and that involves intense effort. Because choosing a chief executive is one of the most important jobs that a chairman has to do.

When a board is appointing a CEO, it is always taking a big risk. For a start, you are almost always faced with the choice of appointing internally or going outside, and both options have significant drawbacks.

The main problem I have with going outside for a chief executive is that their CV might be fantastic and you can take up all the references, but nobody really wants to say negative things about people – so you don't really know how good they will be in the new job. And quite often, it is a step up: they have never been a CEO before and they are advancing their career, or they are moving up from running a smaller company. Either way, they are taking on a bigger job and there is no guarantee that they will be able to meet the challenge.

On the other hand, the issue with internal candidates is that you know their weaknesses. So when you sit down with the non-executive directors, you will explain that he or she is fantastic at this or that, but not very good with investors or tends to keep stuff back from the board, or whatever. Then again, I have had to remind people more often in these situations than not that we know everything about the internal candidate, we know exactly the type of person we are dealing with, whereas if we take on a new person from outside, we don't.

The choice also depends very much on the company's circumstances. If it is in financial trouble, then you need a certain type of chief executive – somebody who will engineer change, make tough decisions and sell businesses, be particularly good at dealing with the banks and shareholders. In that kind of situation, where a company needs change, then you should normally appoint from outside. But you also need to recognise that, if this person succeeds in turning round and stabilising the business, then they are unlikely to be equally well-equipped for the new phase that the company is entering.

They have been very, very active in engineering a corporate recovery and running a steady state business is not necessarily what they are good at. It is not at all unusual for them to become restless and want to go on changing things. In a similar way, you can have someone who is very good at running a business when it is going well but then finds it very difficult to make tough decisions if performance deteriorates. But if 'steady as you go' is what the business needs, then an internal candidate can be the better choice.

Whoever is chosen and whatever the company's circumstances, if that individual is successful the board will eventually have to decide when to replace them. I have very strong views about this issue, because if mishandled it frequently causes much of the chief executive's previous good work to be undone. I have always believed that the maximum period a successful CEO should remain in post is around eight or nine years. By that time, they have done what they have to do and you need a fresh eye.

Many chief executives have stayed too long, and towards the end of their tenure, instead of focusing first and foremost on the challenges facing the business, they start to think about their legacy, how their term will be viewed. And at that moment, they start to put their own interests before those of the company. In such situations, a huge responsibility rests on boards in general and chairmen in particular. Boards can become frightened: they are in awe of the successful chief executive and unwilling to tap him or her on the shoulder and say, "We need to make a change – you have done a great job but we need to move on."

It's sometimes said of me – unfairly – that when I join a board as chairman, the first thing I invariably do is to get rid of the chief executive and install someone I can work with. That's actually not true – it has always depended on the situation of the company, so it has been true in certain circumstances and not in others. There are plenty of examples where I have inherited a chief executive and we have worked very well together. For instance, in two of my most recent chairmanships, I worked happily with Simon Pryce at BBA for several years. Likewise with Stephen Young at Meggitt.

There is no hard and fast rule because each situation is different. In the case of Invensys, I and the rest of the board judged that we needed stability to move the company forward, and we thought Wayne Edmunds would bring that. And that's exactly what he did, as well as proving himself to be an excellent negotiator when we reached the deal-making stage.

14

Invensys, Siemens and Schneider

So, Wayne was appointed and I sat down with him to think about how we should proceed. Invensys was a complex situation but I got to grips with it, and Wayne understood it very well. The external stakeholder relations dimension was new to him but he now had to lead it – with the investors, the analysts and the rest – and I could draw on my deep network of bankers, lawyers, industry and media contacts to help him. Despite the company's difficulties, we worked together well and enjoyed our collaboration.

It didn't take long for the pressure to ratchet up. Within months, we had a profit warning, which wasn't helpful, and at the same time we were getting ever-increasing demands, quite rightly, from Kathleen O'Donovan, chair of the pension trustees, for more money to go into the pension fund. Kathleen was the former finance director of BTR, who had become CFO of Invensys before retiring as an executive.

Because it was so huge relative to the market worth of the company, the pension fund inevitably drove our strategy. I used to really worry about it. Not to the extent of losing sleep over it, because I tend not to do that about any business issue, but it was constantly on my mind because at the end of the day, the chairman is responsible for the pensioners and accountable to them. If the pensioners suddenly had to take a reduction in benefits, they would rightly be looking at me for some answers.

We were having to make considerable contributions to the fund – £40m a year or more – while, to sustain the businesses, we were also compelled to take on riskier contracts. So you could envisage a worst-case scenario where Invensys went into losses, cash drained out of the business and it was unable to continue the level of pension contributions required. At that point, under the accounting rules, a company is on the primrose path to no longer being a going concern. It just was not sensible to carry gross pension liabilities of £5 billion with a market cap. of £1.5 billion to £1.7 billion, which is what we had after the profit warning.

It was clear to Wayne and me that Invensys could not remain in its unsteady state. When Wayne took over as CEO, the free cash flow of Invensys was sufficient to cover the pension contributions, a symbolic and therefore modest dividend, and the bare minimum of re-investment in the three businesses. There was no money for investment in organic growth and none for M&A, unless it was self-funded by disposals elsewhere. Because of the relatively recent rights issue, our access to the traditional capital markets was restricted and/or very expensive. And the clock was ticking: while our three businesses were still solid, if we continued to run them on this very investment-constrained basis, within three to five years we would have badly degraded them, along with the financial coverage for the pensioners.

The pension fund was a real iceberg – only part of it was visible to outside eyes. The sell-side analysts who covered Invensys valued the liability at £700m to £800m, but that was based on the publicly-reported funding deficit. By now, a number of groups with pension fund issues were concluding partial or total buy-outs of the fund with third party insurance companies. But in our case, that was not an easy option: Wayne worked out that the cost of a buyout would be the near-£800m reported deficit, plus about £200m for a risk adjustment to allow for worst-case mortality assumptions for our participants, and another £200m–£300m to provide the third party buyer with the size of profit it would want. So the total cost of a buy-out would be between £1.2 billion and £1.3 billion.

Wayne then identified an alternative solution – instead of negotiating a buy-out of the pension, we could retain it but ensure it was fully funded. That would reduce the total cost, but it still required us to square a circle: to provide security for our pensioners while delivering value to our shareholders.

This was a tricky task, and to achieve it we concluded that we either had to sell the whole company or to divest one of the divisions at a very good price. However, the sale of a division would have huge implications for the pension fund because we would be reducing the size of the company still further relative to the fund. And the combination of the UK's pension governance regulations and the specific terms of the previous Invensys restructuring gave the pension fund enormous power to take large percentages of the proceeds of any disposals – to the detriment of the shareholders, who would have to forego much of the transaction benefit.

As chairman, I was acutely aware of my responsibilities to both stakeholder groups. The cleanest solution would have been a takeover of the whole company, and early on in 2012 we did get a tentative approach from Emerson Electric, a very large American group. Emerson was a world leader in software and control systems and could easily afford Invensys. It had no interest in rail but it could have sold off that division after buying Invensys, thereby recouping a significant chunk of the purchase price.

Emerson met my prime concern – that Invensys should be taken over by a good steward, an owner with the same sense of commitment to the UK pensioner base that we had. But Emerson did not pursue its interest, and I later learned that this was because its board was scared off by our pension fund situation – even though Emerson was so big that it could easily have absorbed the fund without incurring any risk. Emerson missed a great opportunity: it could have snapped up Invensys, whose shares were pretty depressed at the time, auctioned off rail and ended up with the bit it wanted for a very reasonable net outlay.

Anyway, Emerson was out of the picture, and there was no other party interested in the whole business (we had very informal contact with General Electric and one or two Chinese groups, all of which were also worried about the pension situation). Wayne and I therefore had only one solution: we would have to sell a division at an absolutely top price.

We discussed which one of the main businesses – rail or operations management – we should divest and, quite frankly, we could have sold either. We concluded that the more sellable was rail. Although it wasn't an integrated full-line manufacturer, it was a world leader in signalling technology and highly respected internationally. Interest should therefore be strong and the chances of achieving a good price high. Moreover, the global rail industry was consolidating into the hands of a few groups with full-line capability, a trend which presented both opportunity – the chance to maximise the value of our specialist technology – and threat: if we missed the bandwagon, we would be left isolated as a niche player operating at a significant competitive disadvantage which would inevitably erode the value of our business. So we had no time to lose.

We were then approached by China Southern Railways (CSR) which wanted us to form a joint venture with them both in China and worldwide. CSR was first and foremost a rolling stock manufacturer and its signalling and operations software capabilities, compared with ours, were rudimentary.

On one hand, this proposal was encouraging: it bore out our own analysis of the likely level of overseas interest in the business. But we were also extremely wary, because the railway industry in China had a track record of going into joint ventures, stealing the technology, and then abandoning the partnership. This had happened with the Japanese group Hitachi and we knew that was not the only instance. However, we felt it was worthwhile talking to them and I went over to Beijing to meet their senior people.

I told them that, quite frankly, we were not going to agree a joint venture. If they wanted the business, they would have to buy it and that would have to be at a very good price. They agreed to consider this, which was typical: my experience with the Chinese is that they talk and talk and talk but do very little because they are always looking for an opportunity to snap up the technology or the brand they want on the cheap – sometimes even after the business has collapsed. They've done this in a wide range of sectors; Rover cars and Thomas Cook are just two examples. But despite our conclusion that CSR would never pay up for the whole business, we didn't discard them completely. Negotiation is usually a poker game and in this case, the stakes for us were very high.

We now looked at the various other players who might buy the business. We talked to Bombardier of Canada. I had a meeting with Alstom, but they were not really in a financial position to pay. It quite quickly became apparent to both Wayne and myself that Siemens, which of course had almost acquired Westinghouse all those years ago, would be the most likely to pay the price we wanted. Siemens had recently appointed a new chief executive, Peter Loescher, who had previously been at Amersham, the British pharmaceutical company, and then joined America's Merck. He was therefore at home in the world of Anglo-Saxon M&A. He was the first CEO that Siemens had appointed from outside the company and was ready to shake up the risk-averse culture there. He was also an adviser to the boutique investment banking firm Ondra Partners, founded by Michael Tory, the former head of investment banking at Lehman. We therefore appointed Ondra alongside our retained bank JP Morgan to advise us on the sale of the rail business.

I arranged to meet Loescher at Ondra's offices in London. He was clearly a very smooth character and gave nothing away, but I got the impression that he was quite interested in doing a deal with us. A couple of months passed, and then – quite mysteriously and coincidentally, I must say – several stories appeared in the press speculating about a possible sale by Invensys of the rail business to the Chinese. We naturally refused to comment, as one does, but these stories were of course very helpful to us because they concentrated Siemens' mind.

Siemens was terrified of a Chinese rolling stock company acquiring a Western signalling business. As things stood, the Chinese were not globally competitive – no-one in their right mind would want to give a large contract to them involving complex signalling. But that would all change overnight if they bought our business. Then they would become very serious competitors.

Within days of these reports, Siemens contacted us through their advisers to arrange talks. Wayne and I then did some quite detailed work on what rail would be worth to them. We had first-rate technology. We would bring them a commanding position in the UK, which they did not really have. And above all, acquisition would deny the Chinese the chance to buy the last leading independent signalling company, thereby dealing a big blow to their international ambitions. That was worth a lot of money, so we came up with a base number and added 50%–60% to it to account for the value of closing out the Chinese. The Invensys analysts thought rail was worth something over £800m, which with a normal 30% takeover premium equated to a price of up to £1.1 billion. But our hard analysis of rail's business plan financials coupled with the bidding tension between the Germans and the Chinese suggested that, if we played our cards right, we could get around £1.7 billion, which would enable us to satisfy all our stakeholders.

This was all fine on paper – the number we arrived at was very attractive – but our challenge now was to realise it. Wayne did most of the hands-on negotiation and I deliberately remained somewhat detached. I always feel that, in these situations, it is better for the chairman to be in the background and to be called in in the event that there is an apparent impasse – a dispute about the price or some other key aspect of the negotiations.

Wayne turned out to be a fantastic negotiator and we agreed in principle to a price of £1.7 billion, which was enormous and almost larger than Invensys's total stock market worth. We then opened a data room so that Siemens could conduct their due diligence. About two or three weeks into the due diligence process, I got the call that I was expecting from Loescher to say that, on the basis of what they had discovered about the profitability of the business, the nature of the contracts and so on, the numbers didn't work for them and the price was £1.4 billion not £1.7 billion.

I told him that I didn't care whether he made the numbers work; he wasn't going to buy the business for less than £1.7 billion. I put the phone down, talked to Wayne and we withdrew all our team – lawyers, accountants and the rest – from the due diligence. We closed the negotiation down completely. And we waited. Somewhat nervously.

Three or four days later, Loescher came back on the line and said: "You've taken everybody off the deal." And I said: "But Peter, we don't have a deal. I told you what the price was, £1.7 billion. You either pay that or we aren't going to do a deal. And by the way, the Chinese are very, very keen to come to an arrangement with us and if that happens, you know as well as I do, Peter, that they will be competing with you round the world with a modern signalling system. I'm afraid that is the way life is. So you have a one-off opportunity to buy us, or you can forget it."

It was brinkmanship, but this was our one great opportunity to break the shackles that had constricted Invensys for years. Anyway, Loescher came back and said they were prepared to pay our price. Now I had another concern: I had become aware that Siemens' finance director was against the deal because he thought they were overpaying, and I was worried that, if news of the deal leaked, the FD would get support from Siemens shareholders who would balk at the price and kill the sale. In fact, a few months later, there was a boardroom coup in which Peter Loescher was removed and the FD became chief executive.

Thankfully and remarkably – because these things almost always leak to the media – there was no leak. I have very rarely seen a leak that has advantaged a transaction, and in many cases a leak destroys the deal. A classic case was the proposed merger between BAE Systems and Airbus (then called EADS) which was scrapped a few months before the Invensys rail sale to Siemens. I was on the board of BAE for three years and it is my personal view that this deal would have been hugely advantageous to BAE shareholders. But it was killed by a premature leak before all the governments involved had signed up to the transaction.

On 28 November 2012, we announced the sale of rail to Siemens for £1.74 billion. The market cap. of Invensys was only £1.79 billion, so I wasn't surprised to hear that both investors and analysts in the City initially thought that there had been a misprint in the stated price. In fact, this highlighted what I have always believed is a fundamental flaw in how the market generally values companies. Enormous attention is paid to all the financial metrics and ratings that are derived from analyst models of current and forecast performance, but their algorithms seem to be incapable of accounting for a business's strategic position within its industry and therefore its potential value to a buyer.

This flaw has been greatly accentuated by the twenty-first century trends involving ever-increasing sophistication of financial modelling and the rise of automated trading. The analyst community has changed, too. Not so long ago, you would regularly find analysts who understood the companies in your industry – some had even worked in those industries. The best ones knew the people running the companies and the relationships that existed between them. Today, almost all of that has gone. Your average analyst in 2021 is a brilliant mathematician who can manipulate a virtual spreadsheet to the nth degree. But he or she has no feel for the actual business or the industry dynamics.

The same is true of many investors – their decisions are driven by incredibly advanced trading programmes, never by industry feel. Passive, index-based investing – the quant funds, the exchange traded funds (ETFs) – dominates fund management. You end up with an enormous increase in financial data but a huge dearth of industry knowledge. So you are bound to get situations where stocks are significantly mispriced. Of course, for someone who does have industry insight as well as performance data, that creates some great opportunities.

The price we got for rail enabled us to square that circle I talked about. We structured the distribution of the proceeds innovatively, injecting £400 million into the pension fund immediately and creating a 'reservoir trust' of £225 million which could be called on to cover future liabilities. So that was a total of up to £625 million dedicated to our pensioners, which ensured that we would no longer have to make the £40 million-plus of annual contributions. We had eliminated the need for any further funding for at least 15 years.

We returned an equal amount of £625 million to our shareholders through a special dividend. The rest was available to invest in the continuing business. And all this meant that we could at last enjoy normal access to the capital markets. Our shares jumped 27% and one analyst, a long-time Invensys follower, described the price as "an absolute blinder." For the first time in my career, I got letters from investors congratulating me on the deal and Richard Buxton called me personally to thank me and to say that he was sorry he had got it wrong two years earlier over Ulf's departure. Which I took as a nice gesture.

Our judgment that Siemens would be a good owner also proved correct. They established themselves as the global leader in rail infrastructure, invested in the business and enhanced their offer in the UK to the benefit of customers such as Crossrail.

The deal put a stop to the roller-coaster ride that our shares had been on for years. Invensys was now a focused software, systems and controls business with a pension fund which was under control, but it didn't really have a future as an independent company and it was obvious to the market that we were a takeover target.

One impediment to a bid was the external mis-perception of the pension fund. During the negotiations with Siemens, I tried to persuade them to take the pension fund – I offered them a £500 million discount if they would agree to that, so the price would be £1.2 billion not £1.7 billion. I told them that the reason the Invensys pension fund did not show much growth in value was because it had to be very conservatively managed to safeguard our covenant to the pensioners; we had to be totally risk-averse because of the potential impact on the company's ability to pay pensions if asset values dropped. So the fund was entirely invested in low-yielding government bonds; we were effectively prevented from investing in higher-risk, higher-return equities.

I pointed out to Siemens that, within a group of their huge size with the much bigger covenant that they had, the deficit would effectively melt away. It would be easily absorbed and of no consequence to them whatsoever. This was the point at which I knew that the finance director was against the deal, because he put his foot through my proposal. Siemens made a big mistake doing that, because by taking our pension fund, they could have got a big reduction in the purchase price with no risk to themselves.

In the months after the sale, we had incoming calls from two companies interested in buying us. One was Emerson and the other was France's Schneider Electric. Emerson did not push very hard and I assume this was because, even though we had neutralised the pension issue that had previously so worried their board, they could not bring themselves to pay the much higher price that we were now in a position to ask.

Schneider was different. Wayne had a very good relationship with the Schneider people, and their chairman Jean-Pascal Tricoire called him within weeks of the Siemens deal to ask for an introduction to me. I met him and it became apparent that they were the best buyers of the business. We were working together on a wide range of product-specific ventures and we had a similar world view of software's increasing importance as the industrial automation business became dominated by the Internet of Things. So we entered negotiations with them. They liked a number of the businesses and they were really smart, understood the pension fund immediately and realised that the reservoir fund money could be taken straight out if the withdrawal was accompanied by a Schneider guarantee.

We messed around on price for a while and, one Friday late in July 2013, we had a final meeting by the side of Lake Geneva. They wanted to pay just under £5 a share in cash and equity, and we wanted just over £5. There was 10p between us but they weren't moving, we were getting nowhere and I was on the point of giving in and saying OK to 498p when I thought of a little ruse. I said to Jean-Pascal: "Why don't we just halve the difference?" and I held up my right hand. I lost the index finger on that hand years ago in a shooting accident, so I looked at my hand and said to him: "That's not five, it's four – so the price is 502p!" He fell about laughing, then stood up, shook my hand and the deal was done, with an extra £10 million for our shareholders.

And that was the end of Invensys. But it was a good end – much, much better than anyone could have expected when you consider the ill-fated BTR–Siebe merger and everything that had followed. It was one of the best outcomes that I have ever been involved in – it delivered value to our shareholders while safeguarding our pensioners and securing a successful future for each of the divisions.

Schneider subsequently sold the appliance controls business to private equity, where it has prospered under the former Invensys management team. Then Schneider did a very imaginative deal with the UK software and systems business Aveva, injecting its enlarged industrial software division into Aveva in return for a 60% stake in the company, which became a FTSE 100 business.

I give Wayne huge credit for the successful outcome. He was one of the best chief executives I've known, because he understood strategy, he put the interests of the company before himself and as a result he enhanced his reputation. Very rarely do you devise a strategy as he and I did, and then have just about all the blocks fall into place.

15

Heathrow

In the spring of 2007, David Kimbell rang to find out whether I would be interested in becoming chairman of BAA, the airports group that had been taken over the previous year by a consortium led by Spain's Ferrovial for £10 billion. Singapore's sovereign wealth fund GIC and a Canadian investment group were members of the consortium but Ferrovial held 60% and ran the business.

Immediately after the takeover, Ferrovial's chairman Rafael del Pino had become chairman of BAA, but the company had concluded that they should appoint a British chairman due to the political issues involved in BAA. Specifically, they were having some difficulty negotiating with the government and the Civil Aviation Authority (CAA) on the pricing for landing slots at Heathrow.

BAA also owned Gatwick, Stansted, Edinburgh, Glasgow, Aberdeen and Southampton airports but Heathrow was by far its biggest and most valuable asset and was the reason why Ferrovial had bought the business.

I was cautious at first and I told David: "I really don't know why I want to do this." BAA was different from anything else I had taken on because it was so tied up with politics. I had never had anything to do with a business that dealt with the UK government on a day-to-day basis. There was a bit of politics and of course regulation with East Midlands Electricity, but it was nowhere near the scale of BAA.

As I considered the approach, I thought that it would be quite interesting to do something like this, to be involved with government and with a very big, highly regulated business. BAA was a major British company with a very important role in our economy. I was now aged 60 and felt I was ready for this new experience and the different challenges that it would present. So I agreed to see Rafael del Pino, who was the son of Ferrovial's founder, and his representative on BAA's board, a guy called Inigo Meiras. We met at Spencer Stuart's office near Marble Arch.

First off, I quite liked the two of them. They were fairly straight-forward and I asked them about how the business was managed, whether it was well managed or not. They said that they had only been there a year but were reasonably happy with the way it was being run. One particular point prompted my question; I told them that I was getting a reputation for firing chief executives, and I didn't really want a situation where I was going to go in as chairman and have to change the management. They kind of assured me that this was not the case. As I say, they were *fairly* straightforward. But not entirely so.

Then, I made a few enquiries around the place about Ferrovial and how they did business. I went to a series of meetings with the shareholders, including one dinner meeting at the RAC Club in Pall Mall. After all this homework, I decided to go ahead. I negotiated a contract and became chairman in September 2007.

Outside of board meetings, I arranged to meet Rafael and Inigo on a regular basis and within a couple of months I had something quite important to discuss with them. Just in that short time it had become quite apparent to me that, although the BAA chief executive was highly intelligent and worked very hard, he was not really suited to the CEO job.

I said to them: "Look, I don't know what you think, but I just don't think it's going to work with this chief executive." Rafael smiled at me and replied, "Neither do we." So I said: "I thought you assured me you were happy with him?" And Rafael, rather disarmingly, answered: "Well, we didn't think you would take the job if we had told you the opposite!"

So we set about finding a successor. We didn't think there was anyone suitable internally, but, fortuitously, during this period I got a call from Sir John Parker, chairman of National Grid and a director of Airbus, who asked me to meet Colin Matthews. Colin was the former Technical Director of British Airways who had worked for John at National Grid and had recently left the position of CEO at the Severn Trent water company, after successfully trouble-shooting there. This call was a pure coincidence, because John didn't know anything about the BAA situation, but of course I had this reputation for removing chief executives and I was always on the lookout for people who would make good CEOs.

I agreed to meet Colin and we got on extremely well. I liked him enormously: he is not a flamboyant character, but he had good experience of running a public company and he was used to taking tough decisions. The BAA job was high profile and I recognised that Colin was not somebody who enjoyed the limelight, something which became apparent during his tenure. But I thought – correctly, as it turned out – that he would get a grip of the business and I introduced him to the Spaniards, who agreed with me. So we appointed him.

Colin took over just as we opened Terminal 5 at Heathrow, which had cost more than £4 billion. Talk about a baptism of fire. British Airways had decided to move overnight into the new terminal, rather than phasing the move over a period, and we had severe problems with the state of the art computer systems running the baggage handling. Even today, nobody really knows why this was the case, because there had been many dry runs and the problems had not shown up. Some people thought the working practices of the Heathrow unions, who are very powerful, were partly responsible, but there was no hard evidence that was the case.

The opening of Terminal 5 attracted some media interest....
Image: *Private Eye* Issue 1207 © Private Eye. Reproduced with permission.

Anyway, there was massive disruption to passengers with baggage going astray and flights being delayed or cancelled. Of course, it was a complete and utter PR disaster and Colin, almost on his first day, was down there 24/7 sorting the issue out. I spent quite a lot of my time there as well, but I avoided talking to the press.

This almost led to a classic media experience when the *Sunday Times* decided that I must be on holiday. They were about to write a piece basically headlined *Where is Nigel Rudd?*. I got wind of this and did nothing to dissuade them until the Friday night before their deadline. Then I rang up the editor, John Witherow, and said: "Look, I have been at Heathrow all the time, talking to people, talking to passengers, helping with refreshments and so on."

I could sense his disappointment; presumably they had got together pictures of some desert island and me in a deck chair. They still ran a story, along with a picture of Colin and myself as the two people who ruined Easter. Witherow is Rupert Murdoch's longest-serving editor and he is now at the *Times*, which hates Heathrow – maybe it's because he and many of his readers live or have lived in west London and are disturbed by the planes.

My period at BAA put me in mind of the Chinese curse about living in interesting times, along with that Aesop proverb which says you should be careful what you wish for. I had thought BAA would be an interesting experience and I wasn't disappointed. No sooner had we got over the T5 issues than we had to deal with the financial crisis.

All infrastructure companies run with a high level of debt, because they generally produce a steady income stream to service the borrowings. On top of that, Ferrovial had borrowed heavily to finance the BAA acquisition. So we were exposed to the worldwide credit crunch and the British government was very worried that Heathrow might go bust – and then they would have a real problem dealing with the business. So one of the most important things I had to do was to assure the government that we had sufficient funds. It was certainly a serious situation, but our lenders were very, very supportive and we had a really good group of people in our treasury department.

Over the period, we managed to get through although not without a few anxious moments.

But once we'd survived the worst of the financial crisis, we faced a fundamental challenge which was the huge political push to promote competition in UK airports by forcing us to sell three of our seven airports – Gatwick, Stansted and either Edinburgh or Glasgow. We weren't entirely against this idea, but what we totally opposed was the insistence by the government on our putting all these airports up for sale at the same time, in a period where the economy was barely starting to recover from the global crisis.

So we mounted an 18-month rear-guard action to prevent us having to sell all these businesses into a poor market that meant we would be virtually giving the assets away. We went through several appeals, constantly finding holes in the government's argument, but always knowing that at the end of the day, we were going to lose. It was just a question of playing for time in the hope that the market would recover and prices would improve.

Our war of attrition was worth it, because we did manage to prevent a simultaneous fire sale. Nevertheless, we had to put Gatwick up for sale within months and it was sold for £1.5 billion, which was a very, very cheap price at the time. I still find this all quite difficult, because we were a forced seller and the private equity group that bought it made an enormous amount of money from the deal, later selling on half its stake for almost double what it had paid for the whole business. Their timing again proved impeccable, because that was less than two years before the Covid-19 aviation crisis. A couple of years later we sold Edinburgh, followed by Stansted and then Glasgow and Aberdeen, and we got reasonable prices for them.

We were left with Heathrow and renamed the former BAA business accordingly. As chairman of Heathrow, I oversaw our sustained effort to improve the airport's performance and service quality. We had to deal with the fact that it is one of the busiest two-runway airports in the world, if not *the* busiest, that it is restricted to operating for a certain number of hours a day, and that it had one terminal which was really not fit for purpose.

Terminal 5 overcame its teething problems and proved very successful, and following on from that we invested in the new Queen's Terminal that took over Terminals 1 and 2. That was a big improvement and an enormous success. I had the great pleasure of being with the Queen when she opened T5 and then, a few years later, of accompanying her again when she opened the terminal that bore her name. That was the culmination of a decade-long programme in which more than £11 billion was invested in the airport by the private sector. Heathrow is now one of the most modern and efficient airports in the world, but remains severely constrained in terms of capacity. Covid has delayed the need for a third runway, but ultimately that will inevitably be required if Heathrow is not to lose out internationally.

My first involvement in our campaign for expansion was before the general election of 2010, when I met David Cameron at a Conservative fund-raising event in Birmingham while the Conservative manifesto was being developed. I had five minutes with him, during which I begged him not to close any doors in relation to the Heathrow expansion – I told him that I

Receiving an honorary doctorate from
Loughborough University

understood his issue of vulnerable Conservative seats under the flight path, but I said that the alternative options of moving Heathrow to another location, or trying to spread demand over other airports in the south-east, would never be viable economically. I recognised the restrictions that would be put on us in terms of noise and environment, but if we wanted an airport that could serve the national economy and served London, we had to expand Heathrow.

We had quite a short, sharp exchange because Cameron told me categorically that Heathrow would never be expanded, that he totally opposed it and that his manifesto would be specific in reversing the decision made by Geoff Hoon, transport secretary in the Brown government, to allow expansion. I told him that he was wrong and said bluntly that it was stupid to close options down like that. He just waved me away and I didn't really have any contact with him throughout his premiership. We saw each other occasionally from a distance, and he always ran away!

I've seen Cameron since he left office, and he more or less admitted to me that it had been a big mistake not to leave our options open, because we wasted another decade. Eventually, of course, the House of Commons voted overwhelmingly to expand Heathrow subject to certain conditions. Then along came Covid-19, but even during the pandemic it has become clear that airlines like British Airways and Virgin will in the long term focus more on Heathrow, not less.

The other big Tory politician I encountered during this period was Boris Johnson, who was then Mayor of London. I had a number of meetings with him and his advisers. He was of course implacably opposed to expansion at Heathrow – made a famously emotive speech about lying down in front of the bulldozers and so on – and had a crazy idea of moving Heathrow to somewhere in Kent. The 'Boris Island' notion. The phrase that came to my mind was 'Pie in the Sky'.

We tried to explain that if you moved Heathrow, even if that was economically possible, there were three really, really serious practical problems. First of all, you would have to create a town of something like 200,000 people in Kent – simply because that is the number of people who work in and around Heathrow and service Heathrow, in positions that range from hotels to the people directly employed by the airlines and all the rest. Secondly, transport links from the rest of the UK down to Kent would be very difficult with the present infrastructure, so not only would you have to create a new population centre, but you would also need to build new rail and motorway connections. And then there was probably the biggest issue of all: an airport in Kent would create serious problems with international air traffic control, due to its proximity to Amsterdam's Schiphol airport.

We explained all this to Boris Johnson and his team, and I realised very quickly that he is not a man for detail. He had no idea about the specific problems and was not really interested in the arguments. We had a number of discussions with him and/or his advisers and later on, after we sold Stansted to Manchester Airport, he came along to a meeting and said something to the effect of, I have a great idea – I think Heathrow should be moved to Stansted. And since you own the airport, you would benefit financially, just as you would if you expanded Heathrow. I looked at him and said: "Haven't your advisers told you that we have sold Stansted?" And he just stared at me. I concluded that he didn't have any particular view about Heathrow other than he thought, at the time, that to oppose the third runway was a popular thing to do.

Just about the last big thing I was involved in at Heathrow was the appointment of a successor to Colin Matthews. Colin had done six years; it was a tough job with lots of media intrusion and he decided that he wanted to move on. This time we had an excellent internal candidate in John Holland-Kaye, who as development director had led the successful delivery of the Queen's Terminal, and we appointed him chief executive. John is an excellent communicator and a really good leader of people. With John in place, I then handed over the chairmanship to Lord Deighton, an expert in project management who understood the business very well.

I'm very pleased that I agreed to do that nine-year term at Heathrow. As I had anticipated before accepting Ferrovial's offer, it was an experience that I would not have had in a normal private sector business. You are never too old to learn and it undoubtedly enhanced my skill set as a chairman, above all because it taught me a lot about politics and politicians which I might have suspected previously, but had never actually seen at first hand.

People elect politicians to make tough decisions and I think the failure to come to any conclusion about Heathrow is an example of how they can fudge matters for years. I repeatedly tried to point out, to various government ministers, that a construction project of this kind would be enormously helpful to the construction industry, not just in the south of England but all over the country. It was not a question of affordability for the government, because – unlike HS2 and Crossrail or other big projects – all the cost would have been met by private capital. My arguments were to no avail, but in the process I learned all I needed to know about the duplicity of politicians and their unwillingness (for electoral reasons) to make tough decisions. I guess that shouldn't have surprised me, but it did.

16

Business Growth Fund

Of all I have done during my career in business, the Business Growth Fund (BGF) is one of the things I am most proud of, for several reasons.

I trace its origins back to before the general election of 2010, when I had a number of conversations with Lord (Peter) Mandelson and others around the Labour government about the fact that there was a very significant shortage of capital for small and medium-sized (SME) businesses.

In my view, this amounted to a real crisis in funding for Britain's future economic growth. It was a direct result of the financial crisis, because most British SMEs had traditionally used bank finance as quasi-equity. For entrepreneurs, bank loans were relatively cheap and using them meant that you did not have to dilute your interest in the business by giving away equity – something founder-owners were always extremely reluctant to do. Because of the 2008 credit crunch and the near-collapse of the banking system, suddenly this bank finance was either not available at all, or only available on the most onerous terms.

But while the financial crisis had brought the SME funding issue to a head, the roots of the problem dated back decades. I had always felt that if you wanted to grow businesses, you needed very long-term capital and that had been lacking in the UK long before 2008.

Coincidentally, the issue was first highlighted after the most serious economic crisis of the twentieth century, the 1929 crash and ensuing depression, by what was called the Macmillan Committee Report into Finance for British Industry. The government-commissioned report was named after the Scottish lawyer who chaired the committee but largely written by the economist John Maynard Keynes, and it identified what became known as the 'Macmillan Gap' between finance and industry. It contrasted the UK problem with the US and Germany, where finance and industry worked much more closely together.

Immediately after the Second World War, the Bank of England cajoled the British banks into trying to do something about this and they created the Industrial and Commercial Finance Corporation (ICFC) which later morphed into Finance for Industry, Investors in Industry and finally 3i Group. Its remit was to provide long-term capital for small and start-up enterprises throughout the UK, and at its peak 3i had about 26 regional offices. The group also had a huge influence on the nascent British venture capital industry when this really began to develop in the early 1980s – in terms of people, a 3i diaspora developed as managers from the group left to join new VC firms. The British Venture Capital Association (BVCA), which was formed about this time, initially had a nine-person board, of whom four had started on the same day in different 3i offices.

One of the first of the VC firms, Equity Capital for Industry (ECI), was an early investor in Williams and was run by Tony Lorenz, a co-founder of the BVCA. In the mid-1980s, in his book *Venture Capital Today*, he noted a fundamental shift in the nature of the industry away from early-stage investments and in favour of backing management buy-outs (MBOs). There was a simple reason for this, as Lorenz remarked: the risks involved with MBOs were much lower than investing in very young businesses, and the returns could be much higher and come through much faster. And that's absolutely true – investing in early-stage businesses in the hope of making big returns is like looking for a needle in a haystack.

More and more investment funds jumped on the buy-out bandwagon and that's when the venture capital industry became a misnomer. It basically turned into what we now call private equity. Even the hugely-influential 3i abandoned its original remit and, because some of its shareholders like the Midland Bank wanted to cash in their holdings, it went public in the nineties and started chasing the profitable MBO deals.

There was a brief resurgence of start-up funding during the dot. com boom of the late 1990s, but when most of those companies went up in smoke, it disappeared again. So there was already a dearth of capital sources for small businesses when the financial crisis hit, and that wiped out the bits that were left. But I had always been interested in venture capital, and so I had these talks with people around the Gordon Brown government. I believed that, if a source of capital for really small firms was going to be recreated, it would need to be pump-primed with government money because I couldn't envisage anyone in the private sector being interested. So, my aim was to get the government to set up a national fund.

Peter Mandelson asked Chris Rowlands, a former 3i executive, to lead a review into the funding needs of growth businesses, and the Rowlands Report identified that an equity gap existed for UK companies with annual sales between £10 million and £100 million. The report estimated that this was impacting about 25,000–32,000 businesses, of which about 5,000 firms a year were likely to experience significant problems in accessing capital as the economy emerged from recession.

Fortunately, this initiative by Labour was continued by the Conservative–Liberal Democrat coalition government led by David Cameron, which was elected in 2010. I had met Cameron before the general election when he was on one of his visits to the City, and I told him quite bluntly that small and medium-sized companies needed more equity, not more debt. Getting banks to lend more was fine, but in my experience a solid, permanent capital base was essential for growing companies.

A few months after the election, I got a call from Oliver Pawle, UK chairman of the head-hunter Korn Ferry. I had known Ollie for years – before Korn Ferry, he had a long and distinguished corporate broking career at SG Warburg, later UBS. He was close to the Conservatives and knew what they were thinking, and he told me that the new government had started talking to the main British banks about setting up a fund to support SMEs.

The discussions were quite well-advanced and Ollie said the government wanted me to be involved – they had heard that I was interested in this area and with my experience in both industry and finance (I'd come off the Barclays board in 2009), they wondered if I would consider becoming chairman of the new entity. I didn't hesitate – I thought it was something really worthwhile and I was very happy to come in.

We had lots of meetings because there was a huge amount to sort out. Of course, the most important aspect was the funding and the long and short of it was that, since the banks were in such bad odour and needed to rebuild their reputation, their arm was twisted to provide up to £2.5 billion – it was £1.5 billion at first and then another billion was added. These funds would be available for the new entity to draw down over time, as it identified the small firms it wanted to invest in.

The critical thing was getting the Treasury to agree that the banks' investment did not adversely affect their ratios. Normally, if banks take a minority shareholding in something, they have to make a provision covering the whole thing so it can be very disadvantageous for their balance sheet and restrict their ability to leverage. And of course, just as we were doing this, the banking regulators were enormously tightening the restrictions on leverage in order to avoid another financial crisis. So without the Treasury waiver, the banks would have been very reluctant to participate in the BGF. Rishi Sunak ran into similar issues when he was devising the loan support programmes for businesses during the Covid crisis.

The four main clearing banks joined in, together with Standard Chartered who came to the party in a small way. I'll never forget my meeting with Richard Meddings, Standard's finance director. I went to see him to discuss the bank's BGF contribution and he described it as a 'parking fine'. As he saw it, it was just a cost of doing business because the government had forced them to do it and it was to be written off. I think all the banks probably thought that it would just blow up or whatever.

But the government was very committed and did everything they could to make it work. I was very keen, despite the fact that it originated in a government initiative, that there should be no ongoing government involvement in the running of the BGF. I felt that it would have the best chance of success if it was to operate independently and without any sense that it could be subject to state intervention. The government accepted that key principle.

With that potential hurdle removed, we formed a board whose non-executive directors included a number of representatives of the shareholder banks. The most important thing then was to identify the right chief executive. And we came across Stephen Welton. Stephen had started life as a banker and then moved into private equity, where he founded JP Morgan's PE arm (now called CCMP Capital). His credentials were outstanding and he has gone on to do an amazing job in building the business.

The BGF first surfaced in October 2010, as a 37-word sentence in the government's Business Finance Taskforce report, which outlined 17 measures to be taken by the big UK banks to help the UK recover from the recession. The following February the chancellor, George Osborne, formally announced it as part of Project Merlin, the government's wide-ranging reformation plan for the post-crisis banking sector which encompassed bank lending to business, a clampdown on bank bonuses, and increased transparency in executive pay.

We started with two offices, in London and Birmingham, and officially launched the Fund on 19 May 2011 in Birmingham. This was deliberate because we wanted to send a signal: Stephen and I were very keen to ensure that we backed firms all over the country, unlike many funds which were south-east England-centric.

The launch's theme was 'confidence, collaboration and capital for growth'. It took place at a time when the UK was just emerging from the financial crisis recession. The story – in the Midlands and elsewhere – was one of renewal and regeneration. People had to pick themselves up, dust themselves down and carry on with optimism. The BGF was one of the very few pluses to come out of a very difficult economic situation. I'm sure Stephen bore that in mind when in late 2020 he made a very strong case for government action to support growth businesses in the wake of the Covid crisis.

I described us as talent-spotters for UK plc. We aimed to invest in firms within the £10m–£100m annual sales range, injecting between £2m and £10m in return for minority equity stakes and a seat on the board. However, we determined that our criteria would not be set in stone – our real focus was on the investee company's growth potential and the strength of its management team and business plan. And as I said at the launch, we looked for returns which were "fair and reasonable, not rapacious and onerous."

Perhaps the most important point was to convince our audience that we really were something different, something that had not previously existed in the marketplace. I recognised that it could take some time for companies to adjust to this and to work out how they could successfully use the investment and expertise that we would offer them. And I was also careful to acknowledge that many of the companies that did approach us would not meet our investment criteria: "We are expecting to kiss many frogs before finding our princes and princesses."

From the outset, we adopted a 'patient capital' investment strategy, which immediately made us exceptional in the UK industry. We took minority, non-controlling stakes in our investee companies with the aim of retaining those holdings over a long period, rather than just for the three-to-five years commonly targeted by your average PE firm. We didn't have to pay dividends to our investors, the banks – we could reinvest the returns we made. We never pressured our companies to produce short-term profit growth and the level of returns demanded by conventional PE.

This long-termism helped us overcome the natural reluctance of many SME founders to cede part of their equity interest to an outsider. And we also took a significant stake in the management: we always insisted on putting someone on the board and we almost always appointed the chairman. Our firms saw that this made them more bankable: it gave the banks and the other stakeholders dealing with these young companies – including suppliers and customers – much greater confidence in their financial stability and their future viability.

Everyone involved with early-stage businesses knows that their mortality rate is very high, so until we came along, if you had a company which wanted to grow, and you went along to the bank and asked to borrow some money for working capital, the bank would say, "Well, it's quite difficult." But if you went along and said "BGF has a stake in us," then the bank knew the company had a more secure capital base and became much more confident about lending to it. And as the banks took this on board, and we became recognised as the primary UK source of equity capital for the early-stage business community, they started to refer companies to us.

Stephen and I complemented each other in terms of strengths and experience, arriving at the same place from different starting-points. Stephen was a venture capital professional and, through Williams, I had been both entrepreneur and a client and recipient of VC investment. My Barclays period meant that I knew exactly how banks think and why they are so cautious about backing early-stage firms – apart from anything else, that kind of commercial lending is inherently unprofitable and the bad debt rates are sky-high. So I could speak the language of both the banks that were backing us and the small company owners we were backing.

Until venture capital came along, the banks were effectively holding quasi-equity in many of these small firms, with no ability to influence management because as soon as they would start to try and exert some influence, they were seen as having a conflict of interest with their position as a lender. We provided the banks with a superb way of being involved in supporting small businesses without all the problems they were used to, and they knew that, if a company did get into some kind of trouble – if the cycle moved against them, for instance – then there was somebody else behind it.

We were both quite astute politically, which was important given BGF's provenance. Initially, we faced suspicion and even hostility from some of the established private equity firms, who saw us as a competitive threat. Our willingness to take minority stakes and our long-termism certainly made us more attractive to investee companies than conventional PE firms were.

Tim Hames, director-general of the BVCA at the time, recalled that some members initially opposed his desire to invite us into the association, which we were happy to join. Stephen and I recognised the issue and made it very clear to the PE community that we were not in the business of eating their lunch. In a few cases where we were interested in investing but discovered that another PE firm was already in negotiations with the company concerned, we held back. But because of our particular target market and our nationwide coverage, we did not encounter such potential conflicts very often.

Building a genuinely national network was, from day one, among our major differentiating factors: with a few exceptions, the PE industry was south-east England-centric. BGF now has at least 14 offices in the UK covering all regions and countries, together with two in the Republic of Ireland. In a way, we became what ICFC was intended to be before it gradually abandoned its original role. It wasn't exactly wizardry – it was down to perspiration as much as inspiration – but we lived up to the Merlin name. Our national mission has helped create a virtuous circle, because we have grown deep roots across the small business community and created one of the most amazing networks of accessibility to individuals – we have a huge database of people who are willing to come in to investee firms, maybe as a finance function or to be our representative as chairman. And we quite like these men and women to take a bit of a stake in the business, as well.

The Irish presence is a direct result of BGF's success in the UK: imitation is the sincerest form of flattery and, after we had been running a few years, their government came to us and asked us to run their own Strategic Investment Fund, which had up to 250 million euros to invest and was backed by their main banks. Many other countries, including Australia and Canada, have come to us over the years to ask about the blueprint for setting up similar funds.

By volume of deals, we have actually become the world's most prolific VC investor. Our investment range has been slightly wider than we originally envisaged – it varies between £1 million and £20 million - but the average is about £7m to £8m. That usually translates into 20% to 25% of the business – it could be less; it could be more. We invest in a whole range of sectors – about the only ones we avoid are financial services, to ensure we have no conflict with our investors the banks, and property. Other than that, we are in virtually every area of manufacturing and services. We've got about 15,000 companies on our database; we meet about 2,000 each year, make about 200 proposals, and complete about 50 investments.

Because the fund is not time-limited, unlike almost all PE funds, we can follow on with really good companies which are expanding and need more money to finance that growth. That tends to lead to our best investments, because we know the company inside out, we know exactly what the money is for, we know the management will use it well and so the outcome is very, very good. Of course, we have had failures but that is inevitable in this line of work.

I decided to step down in 2020 after nine years, and Stephen became executive chairman. By then, we had invested almost all the original £2.5 billion fund in more than 300 companies – getting on for two-thirds of that total in businesses headquartered outside London and south-east England. We were starting to make a good profit and the banks who backed us at the start saw BGF as an asset, not a contingent liability: it's not the best investment they ever made because the returns are not as high as in some other cases, but it is certainly not the write-off that many of them thought it would be. It is a great formula – the primary source of equity capital for new and small businesses in the country. So it is actually achieving something that otherwise would never have happened, and the UK economy would have been very much the poorer without it. That's why I'm so pleased to have played a part in its success.

17

Signature

The takeover of Invensys freed me up to take another board position, if something interesting came along. And that actually happened very quickly, within a few months of the Invensys deal.

The company concerned was BBA, a mini-conglomerate which had been one of the many holding companies that developed in the wake of Hanson, BTR and Williams in the 1980s. In fact, when I was at Williams we had bought a fire protection business called Angus from BBA which became part of Kidde. And just to complete the circle, the chairman of BBA who asked me to come in was Michael Harper, who had been my chief executive at Kidde.

Michael had joined BBA as a non-executive director after Kidde was taken over, and had stepped in as emergency chief executive when the then-CEO fell ill. Then Roberto Quarta, BBA's long-standing chairman, stepped down at short notice and Michael succeeded him. For a period he was both chairman and CEO, before recruiting Simon Pryce to become chief executive. Michael was coming up to retirement and, along with the head-hunter Jan Hall, was instrumental in persuading me to join the BBA board as a prelude to becoming chairman.

I had other good connections with the company, because I was an old friend and business partner of Roberto, who was then chairman of the engineering company IMI and a partner at the private equity firm Clayton, Dubilier and Rice (CDR). He later became chairman of the medical equipment company Smith & Nephew and WPP, the advertising business. And after the Invensys sale, Wayne Edmunds had joined the BBA board and the other directors also wanted me to come in. So altogether I would be joining a group of people I knew and liked and admired. I became a director a few months before Michael's retirement and was then appointed chairman.

I thought BBA looked quite interesting because it had some structural issues which needed sorting out. Under Roberto, it had made an audacious attempt to take over Lucas, which was one of the historic names in the British motor components industry. That failed, so he sold BBA's auto business and later spun off BBA's industrial textiles arm. He identified private aircraft services as a growth business and through acquisition, built up a network of flight support bases mainly in the US which formed a highly-profitable division called Signature. By the time I became chairman, Signature was the largest of four divisions, all in the civil aviation industry but unrelated to each other. The others were an aero-engine repair and overhaul (ERO) business, Ontic – a very profitable unit which made parts for older, 'legacy' aircraft – and an airport services division called ASIG.

I got on well with Simon Pryce, who had come to BBA from the engineering group GKN. He was originally an investment banker, one of the few who has been successful in industry. He had joined GKN in 1997 as head of corporate finance and strategy, and moved up through the CFO ranks to run one of the group's divisions.

Simon and I shared the view that ASIG, which included baggage handling, refuelling and de-icing, was a horrible business with really unattractive cashflow dynamics. Simon hadn't sold it earlier because it was the one area of the business that didn't suffer a massive downturn during the financial crisis. Signature was hard hit because business aviation fell off a cliff –bankers were no longer jumping on private jets to do deals. But commercial aviation held up, so ASIG's cash flows sustained BBA for a couple of years until Signature recovered.

We concluded that ASIG should be sold as soon as we could do a sensible transaction at a reasonable price. Baggage handling basically involves selling blue collar labour hours and effective labour organisation. It is all about scale at an airport – hugely labour-intensive and employing thousands of people. Contracts with the airlines are short-term, barriers to entry are very low, everything is priced off variable cost and the margins are therefore slim.

To make matters worse, it is also capital-intensive because much of the handling, refuelling and de-icing equipment is owned by the operator. And every time one of your trucks nudges an aircraft, that creates an insurance claim. After a number of false starts and a very protracted negotiation, we sold ASIG to another industry incumbent, John Menzies. The price wasn't great, but the important thing was to improve the quality of our portfolio.

That disposal cleaned up BBA and removed a lot of its complexity because it left us focused on the three remaining businesses. It was clear to me that ultimately we should separate them, but first we had to grow Signature further because the benefits of scale in that business were very significant.

Whilst we had been successful in improving operational performance and in finding a number of bolt-on acquisitions, the flight support industry contained three major players when it was clear that, in order to maximise the returns, there should only be two. I therefore advised Simon to look at the acquisition alternatives, telling him: "Work out what you want to buy, how much you are going to pay and then go and get that company."

Simon had always wanted to do the big deal for Signature and appreciated what he called my encouragement to take "managed risk" to balance risk and reward. Part of getting that balance right is down to intuition, which you can't really teach. Experience helps – as long as you learn from it. But you can certainly encourage your CEO and their team to assess risk without just avoiding it in any situation and at all costs. You will never achieve anything if you hunker down like that. I simply said to the executive team: think about this company as if it was your company and ask yourselves how you would create value. And never forget that the best gauge of the quality and strength of a business is sustainable cash generation.

Simon soon identified his prime target. Apart from Signature, the other two main operators were Atlantic Aviation, owned by the private equity firm Macquarie, and Landmark Aviation, which had been bought a few years earlier by the PE firm Carlyle. Simon had looked at buying Landmark before it was sold to Carlyle, and now he approached Carlyle with an offer. Atlantic were also interested, and Simon had some discussions with them about whether we should join forces to buy Landmark and then break it up, but in the end he decided to go it alone and I completely agreed with that. We were now in what was effectively an auction and that meant we would have to pay a pretty full price to win.

I left Simon and his team to handle the deal and provided some guidance and input when requested. Both Simon and I thought that it would be worth paying up in order to win the competition, because the combination with Signature would generate substantial value. In the end, we agreed to buy Landmark for $2.1 billion. Simon and his team produced a detailed integration plan which I reviewed, and the acquisition proved every bit as value-creative as we had anticipated.

I believe that most CEOs are at their best in years three to seven of their tenure, and Simon agrees with me. When I became chairman, I asked him: "How long will you give me?" And he said that he planned to stay another year to 18 months. Landmark changed that because, as I told him bluntly: "You've got to stay here to oversee the integration and if that goes wrong, I'll fire you." To which he replied: "Thank you very much!"

Because so much of the business was based in the US, the integration effort meant that Simon had to spend an enormous amount of time there. He was basically living in Florida for about two weeks in every month, and that was also putting a lot of pressure on his home life. About 18 months after the acquisition, with the Landmark integration successfully completed, Simon and I had a discussion and decided that it was the right time for him to hand over the reins. Simon went on to become CEO of Ultra Electronics, the defence technology group, and he is doing a fantastic job there.

I am very pleased for him – we speak regularly and maintain a close relationship.

We appointed Wayne Edmunds, whom I knew to be a very safe pair of hands, as interim chief executive while we conducted an extensive search for Simon's successor. We looked inside, where Simon and I had already identified three strong candidates, and outside, and at the end of the day we appointed the leading internal candidate, Mark Johnstone. Mark had had a number of roles in BBA including running Signature Europe and culminating in running ERO, and he established his base in Orlando, which made a lot of sense given the US weighting of the group.

Before Mark took over, BBA had been in talks to buy a big repair and overhaul business in the Middle East, but I called those negotiations off because I didn't like that business – I didn't think we had any real competitive advantage in ERO, which is a crowded market where so long as you have the basic expertise you just sell on price. The main customers are big aero-engine manufacturers like Rolls-Royce and Pratt & Whitney, and they basically dictate the terms of trade so you can never be master of your own destiny. I've always believed that if you are going to have a successful business, you have to have some competitive advantage. That sounds a truism, but you'd be surprised how many companies stay with businesses that don't have any edge and therefore struggle for growth.

Ontic was different: Michael Harper had bought it and it was an amazing business occupying a very profitable and cash generative niche in the civil aircraft market where the barriers to entry are high. It buys end of life rights to produce parts for old jets – planes that are still flying but in very small numbers so that it is uneconomic for the big component manufacturers to continue to make those parts. These parts are of course safety-critical, and they all have to be certified. The cost of certification is huge, so by and large many of these products are either single- or dual-sourced. And when you are replacing a part, you cannot use a part which hasn't been certified. Therefore you have a captive market to a certain extent at least.

You cannot overstate the emphasis on safety in the aerospace business, which is why much of the industry involves products and services that are high-margin and high-value. This does not however apply to all of commercial aviation. I've been involved in many different parts of it over the years, and one thing I have learned is that the further away you get from actually operating the aeroplane, the more money you make. The second-tier manufacturer of a widget which is vital to a Boeing or Airbus aircraft makes huge margins, whereas American Airlines or WizzAir or whatever airline you choose to name are always being hit by cyclical factors.

McKinsey, the management consultancy, once did a survey which showed that, over the past 40 or 50 years, the commercial aviation industry overall had destroyed rather than created value. The only segment within the industry that had made good money was the tier two manufacturers. But the gains that carriers made during peak periods were more than wiped out by the cyclical troughs. The problems posed by Covid are of a different order of magnitude from the difficulties in your average cyclical downturn, but they certainly haven't changed the fundamental reality that airlines are not a great commercial proposition.

On the other hand, the strict regulatory requirements can create significant growth opportunities elsewhere in the industry. When I was chairman of Kidde, a plane came down in the Florida Everglades because there was a fire in the cargo hold caused by some gas canisters. After that crash, the fitting of fire detection and suppression systems in cargo holds became mandatory, which had not been the case before, so that one incident drove a huge increase in demand for Kidde products.

BBA had got into the Ontic business in 2006 when it bought a company for about $67 million. Simon and the team had expanded it over the years by investing another $300 million in acquiring or licensing the underlying intellectual property to more and more parts on legacy platforms from the original equipment manufacturers. It was such a successful model and Ontic became so valuable that in 2019, we were able to agree a deal to sell it to the private equity firm CVC for almost $1.4 billion. We returned $835 million (about £670 million at prevailing exchange rates) of that price to our shareholders, and the share price went to more than 390p – it had been just under 280p when I became chairman.

Why did we sell it at all, given that it was so profitable and still growing? There I come back to the nature of conglomerates. I have been chairman of several during my career and, to be successful, you needed to be large-scale. If something went wrong in one or two parts of such a group, you wanted to have 10 different divisions and you were basically a portfolio manager. To be a conglomerate with just two or three unrelated companies underneath the holding structure is just a nonsense, because the group as a whole is simply not large enough and problems in one area can pull the whole lot down. That's why, once the move to divest divisions took hold, the conglomerates had no future except as focused pure plays.

Capital allocation is the crucial factor. You have to make capital decisions based on the availability of capital. If you have two or three unrelated businesses, you are constantly having to choose which one to invest in, whereas if you own only one, then you are automatically making a capital investment decision for the whole company.

Interestingly, one of the most telling points I have ever heard from a non-executive director was made by a NED at BBA when we were discussing whether we should keep Ontic. She said: "The moment we decide that we are not going to invest in parts manufacturing licences because we have to spend more money on Signature is the day we should sell Ontic." In other words, once you have to start making these choices of capital allocation then the business that misses out should be sold, because it needs to be owned by someone who is prepared to make that investment to take it forward. Her comment reinforced my view that Ontic would be better owned by someone else.

In fact, because of the need to fund Ontic's expansion, we reached a moment when we faced the prospect of having to use cash generated by Signature to invest in Ontic. This didn't make sense, since Signature was the heart of the business, and it didn't go down well with investors, who bought our stock primarily because of Signature's growth prospects.

After we sold Ontic, we renamed the group Signature and started the process of selling ERO, the final step in turning the company into a pure play. Signature now has the world's largest network of private aviation hubs, which enables it to leverage economies of scale in areas such as procurement. It is one of the largest purchasers of aviation fuel in the world.

The extent of Signature's growth will depend a little bit on how private aviation develops – historically, it has grown roughly around GDP rates, but one of the things we have to consider is whether there will be a backlash against the sector because of the increase in environmental awareness. However, biofuels already exist and are being further developed, and they will replace kerosene. They are currently expensive, but the price will come down.

Growing the business over the long term will be very straightforward – you can scale up by adding more bases in different geographies – and it is highly cash-generative, because most of the sites are leased and you get paid by the aircraft operators before you pay anything out. So the income stream is very good. It's a really sweet business and I always thought that private equity would eventually recognise that. I have described Signature as an unregulated utility, and as such it should be able to carry a great deal more debt than our UK shareholders would ever countenance. And being a predominantly US-based business, the logical place for it to be quoted would be New York.

The board were very well aware that, in selling Ontic, we had made ourselves attractive to private equity. Our job was to run the business well, and certainly Mark Johnstone and his team were doing just that. Quite frankly, we then had to wait for the inevitable call.

It came initially in early 2020 from the boutique investment bank Gleacher Shacklock. Would I meet with two executives from Blackstone (one of the largest PE firms)? I agreed. Mark and I met them in London and they expressed an interest in buying Signature. This was before the pandemic, and they then came up with two offers that were way below our expectations, so the board rejected them. We then did a major piece of work on how much a PE buyer could pay for our business. At a stretch, we concluded that anything approaching £4 billion would be difficult to refuse.

During the spring/summer of 2020, everything went quiet. On the stock market, our share price slumped to 185p, its lowest level for many years, because the City thought that we were suffering badly from the pandemic. In fact, the private jet business in the US proved relatively resilient, because it offered customers an accessible alternative to scheduled air travel which was problematic and beset by restrictions to services. By December, business jet travel had recovered to 95% of the level in December 2019. The undervaluation highlighted yet again the insularity of the London market: UK-based analysts had no idea what was really happening in the US business.

The same was not true of Blackstone, who knew exactly what was going on in the American economy. Towards the end of the year, they came back with a bid which was near enough to our aspiration that we allowed them to start due diligence. It was in US dollars, and we agreed to work in that currency.

Next, I got a call from Bayo Ogunlesi, the head of Global Infrastructure Partners (GIP), the PE firm that had bought Gatwick Airport in 2009. He told me that they were about to send me a letter offering to buy Signature. Their bid was below Blackstone's, so the board rejected it immediately.

However, just before Christmas the possibility of a bid leaked to the media and we made an announcement that we were in talks with Blackstone. No sooner had we done this than Carlyle – from whom we had bought Landmark Aviation – appeared, also expressing an interest in Signature. So we now had no fewer than three major potential PE bidders, all of whom understood the business well.

I always knew that our largest shareholder would have a big say in what happened to the company. This was Cascade, the investment company controlled by Bill Gates, which held 20% of our equity. During my chairmanship, I had many conversations with Cascade about the business, and I knew that they were very reluctant to sell. They were absolutely key, because most bids would require a 75% shareholder vote in favour and this would be almost impossible to achieve without the support of Cascade.

It therefore came as no surprise to me that, on 8 January 2021, Blackstone announced that they were teaming up with Cascade. We all thought that this was game, set and match – but GIP then took the really brave decision to raise their bid. We accepted their offer, which was higher than Blackstone's, even though we knew that they would find it very difficult to get the requisite 75% support. Our share price climbed to an all-time high of 421p. Then in a final twist to the saga, GIP joined forces with Blackstone and Cascade and in early February the trio topped up the offer price to $5.62 a share, which valued us at almost £3.5 billion.

The winning offer meant that, along with the capital return from the Ontic sale, we had delivered very substantial value to our shareholders. I think we obtained a great price, despite starting with the fundamental disadvantage that companies listed in London continue to be seriously undervalued in comparison with those quoted on Wall Street. This is a long-standing fact of corporate life and helps to explain why, over the years, so many UK businesses have fallen prey to US takeovers. We got a premium to the undisturbed share price of almost 60%, which clearly demonstrates the US–UK valuation gap and is way above the average premium paid for UK companies, both historically and now. The rating disparity was even more obvious and more critical in relation to Meggitt, for reasons I will explain later.

I don't think I have ever chaired a board where, when I left, the share price hasn't been higher than when I started. In some cases that has been through the company being acquired; in others, through growth or demerger. I'm very proud of that record because, ultimately, increasing shareholder value has to be the acid test for a board of directors.

18

Meggitt

The year after I became chairman of BBA, I was minding my own business when I was contacted by a leading investor in Meggitt, one of the UK's larger aerospace companies. I knew Meggitt from Williams days; it was nowhere near the size of BAE Systems or Rolls-Royce, but it was one of a very small group of UK suppliers which were only one level down from those giants. It was a fine company, particularly strong in braking systems for both commercial and military aircraft, with a history dating back to the early years of post-war aerospace.

However, the investor who called me said the company was extremely introverted and asked me if I knew that it was looking for a new chairman. I said I hadn't heard that. He went on to say that some of the major shareholders were concerned that it was about to run a closed process and appoint from inside the existing board, whereas they wanted an external person. He then asked if I would consider being put forward by this investor group.

I told him that I didn't really need another chairmanship. But I was curious, so I asked if I could talk to any other investors. And he said that M&G were very keen for me to get involved, so I made an appointment to see them. They had been shareholders for a long time and they took me through the whole Meggitt story – they thought it was a great company but it just needed an outsider as chairman who had my kind of background and knowledge of the industry, and who would be prepared, if necessary, to make changes.

After hearing all this, I said that I would consider it. The next step was that one of the investors got hold of the head-hunter, Luke Meynell, and asked him if he had Nigel Rudd on the list. Of course, he said he did – I don't know whether that was true or not, but he probably would have had to say that anyway!

Luke had done some work for me at Heathrow as well as for the Business Growth Fund. He called me and asked if I was interested in Meggitt, and I said that I was but that there was a real difficulty which he needed to understand. Putting myself in the place of a non-executive director, I knew that if I was on a board and a shareholder told us: "You have to have this person as chairman," then we would probably be quite nervous and would resist the appointment. So I told Luke very clearly that if I was to become chairman, it had to be with the unanimous support of the board. To be imposed on the board by some shareholders would be a nightmare situation for everyone.

Luke is a very skilled operator and he told me that I should meet Stephen Young, Meggitt's chief executive, and see how I got on. Our paths had first crossed about 25 years earlier when he was handling the disposal of a number of Thorn EMI's non-core activities, and Williams bought their fire protection business which we later merged with Chubb. He remembered me too, and we had dinner.

Stephen had been CEO for about two years, having previously been finance director for nine years. So he was closely involved with Meggitt's development over that period. He knew my reputation for getting rid of chief executives and he said to me half-jokingly, quoting something from one of my press interviews: "Well, you say that you back your CEOs 100% until you can't support them anymore, and then you fire them immediately. So you will be put in to sack me, won't you?" And I said, equally directly: "I am not going to come here and sack you on day one. My first port of call would be to spend some time looking at the business and making sure it was all being run properly and so on. If I am chairman, I have got to make sure that the shareholders and everyone are content that I am doing the job thoroughly." And he basically said, "fair enough."

That was crucial, because I think that if Stephen had said to the board, "I'm terrified of Nigel coming in, he is going to fire me," then there would have been real difficulties. He obviously talked to the NEDs, and then I met them individually and I liked them. There was Guy Berruyer, former chief executive of the software group SAGE, and Paul Heiden, who had been finance director of Rolls-Royce, and the others. And I got on with them very well. I said I really liked the business, but I felt that in some senses it was trying to hide itself away. It was based down in Bournemouth and kept a very low profile considering how significant a company it actually was. As a company, it never even spoke to the media, didn't have any contacts, didn't tell people about the important things it was doing.

I told the directors that I thought Meggitt needed to raise its profile considerably, not merely for PR purposes but because if it didn't, it would either be sold cheaply to someone bigger or it would simply never fulfil its potential. Its position and prospects as one of the UK's major aerospace systems producers were not widely recognised and therefore nowhere near fully-valued.

The directors all agreed with this approach, so I said that I would join the board, that I wanted to spend some time looking at the management team but also – unusually for me, because I don't normally interfere with appointments of advisers – that we had to run a proper beauty parade for financial public relations advisers. They had had the same PR adviser for years, but it was a specialist in smaller companies. I told Stephen that I wanted him and his people to get out and talk about the business more.

Meggitt was going through a difficult time. They had had two profit warnings before I joined, and the City was just waiting for another one. It has this adage about profit warnings coming in threes, which has proved remarkably accurate more often than not. Sure enough, about six months after I joined, we had another profit warning. Which was a setback.

Meggitt had been run pretty hot for some time, in the sense that a few years earlier it had carried plenty of fat and Stephen and his team had cut that back and eliminated a number of the 'soft' reserves in the business. There then came a stage when there was nothing left to cut back and this coincided with a downturn in trading due to two factors, one a short-term quality issue in one area of activity and the other a more fundamental change in the nature of Meggitt's maintenance business which impacted demand for its highly-profitable spares.

Specialist third-party maintainers of aircraft had been moving into the commercial aerospace market using big data technology to catalogue every part of an operator's fleet. This was creating a double whammy: it made possible the precise identification of faults, so that instead of buying a replacement part you could repair the existing one, and it was increasing preventative maintenance – anticipating equipment failures so you could carry out pre-emptive repairs.

All in all, this trend was extending the life of parts and therefore reducing demand for the spares that Meggitt historically supplied. These spares were sold at margins well into double digits, so the structural shift was hurting Meggitt and they had to adapt. Stephen and his team had developed an 'if you can't beat them, join them' plan which essentially meant adopting the business model of these independent competitors and becoming the sole provider and maintainer of those parts originally made by Meggitt. It was a good strategy but it was not a quick fix and it was clear that we weren't going to make the expected numbers for the year. So we had to say something to the City and of course, that was very difficult.

Stephen was now convinced that I would fire him, and I had a long conversation with him. He is someone I came to like and admire, and I said to him: 'Look, Stephen – I am going to support you. I have only been here six months and I have seen nothing that would justify replacing you with somebody else. You are making some good changes to the management; you are doing a lot of the right things. So I am going to see this through with you and give you air cover." So I went out and dealt with the shareholders, who were obviously unhappy.

I've been involved in investor relations (IR) from the earliest days with Williams, and over the years, that part of my job has become increasingly complex and challenging. The main reason for this is the vast growth of regulation. I understand why the world has moved on from the early 1980s, but in those days you could communicate in a very open way with the owners of your business, and that was hugely useful both in avoiding surprises for them and in being able to seek their advice on how the business should expand, what level of debt was appropriate and what acquisitions were either feasible or advisable.

The internationalisation of fund management has also made a huge difference. Once upon a time, a UK management team could cover most of its key investors via a two-day walk around the square mile in London and perhaps a day trip to Charlotte Square in Edinburgh. The emergence of the truly global investment behemoths, the ascension of hedge funds, the explosive growth from the Far East and the continued rise of sovereign wealth funds demand a much more proactive and dynamic approach to investor relations.

Moreover, the likes of BlackRock and Capital can be difficult to navigate because they incorporate so many different funds, with differing strategies, research structures, underlying mandates and demands. And of course, financial criteria are no longer their be all and end all. Inside the new mantra of ESG – environmental, social and governance – environmental policy and action is a vast area, and so is the ever-increasing attention paid to corporate governance. Some investors are now deciding whether to accept a takeover bid not just because of the price they are being offered, but because they approve or disapprove of the target company's record on governance.

In this context, it is vital that companies are proactive, taking the initiative, asserting a leadership role in governance and ensuring our agenda is aligned with our strategic and business goals. This requires a fresh approach to investor relations and increases the importance of the IR function within a company, certainly from my perspective as chairman. I seek early warning signs from the IR team of any significant issues on the horizon. Early warning signs allow the board to be more proactive, attempting to address or further explain a position before it reaches a crunch point with shareholders. Because amid all the changes in IR that have taken place over the past 40 years, one thing remains absolutely fundamental: the key test of any institutional relationship is whether it can be called upon at a time of need for the company.

After my meetings with the Meggitt shareholders, I gave Stephen a full and honest picture of where he stood with the investors – that no matter how good a performance he put in in the future, his card was marked. The fact that he had been there for many years, first as finance director and then CEO, also counted against him: they wanted change at the top. I acknowledged that and Stephen recognised it too. He already had plans to 'go plural' – to step down from Meggitt at the right time and move into the world of non-executive directors. So we agreed that we would get through this period of turbulence and then plan for the succession. Which we did.

What I had come to appreciate fully was the phenomenal base of positions that Stephen and his team had built up over a number of years through their presence on virtually all the new aircraft that had been developed by the Americans and Europeans. They had stuck to this course through thick and thin – the profit warnings – and there was no doubt that they had done the right thing.

Many investors did not appreciate this achievement – for instance, we were criticised by a number of US shareholders for the amount we had capitalised as research and development on the balance sheet. These investors thought it was just an accounting device to bolster profits, but actually it was a true and fair reflection of the future worth of these 'ship set' positions – the value of the systems that the company had on each platform. As a result of this investment, Meggitt products were embedded in a host of new generation commercial and military aircraft from Airbus and Boeing jets to the F-35 Lightning, the Joint Strike Fighter. Not only were we on more aircraft types than before, but where we had been present on older models, our content on their successors was much greater.

All this added up to a guaranteed rich seam of future cash flow for the company. An aircraft programme can run for around 50 years from start to finish – the daddy of them all is the American B-52 bomber, which has been going for 90 years. In the first five years – which is where Meggitt was at the time on a number of programmes – you are investing in R&D so you are suffering both a cash outflow and making a loss on the business. Then you have a period of about a decade when the fleet is building up so you are supplying OE parts but at low margins – therefore the cash flow turns positive, but the profits are small. After about year 15, you are both supplying more OE parts at ever-increasing margins with economies of scale, and getting a rising income from spares and servicing. That's when you get the big payback.

The cash and profit trajectory works like an annuity. What you are effectively building through the up-front investment is a very long-term and hugely profitable legacy. And that's what Stephen's team had created, particularly in Meggitt's brakes business, where it had a fantastic global presence in areas such as business and regional jets. They deserved huge credit for that.

Stephen and I got on well. I valued what he was doing and he appreciated my willingness to let him get on with it while being available whenever he needed my advice. We also had some funny moments – including one on a tour round our US plants when I nearly missed an internal flight: I had been ahead of him in the queue to board, but when he got on the plane I wasn't there. They were about to push back from the gate when he looked out of the window and saw me sprinting across the tarmac. American airports are like UK bus terminuses – there are a lot of stands close together and I had got on the wrong plane before realising my mistake just in time. Stephen thought that was highly amusing.

One American fund that did appreciate the latent value in Meggitt was Elliott, which is best known as an activist, a corporate raider, but also has an investment management arm. They bought 5% to

6% of the business through contracts for difference (CFDs). Elliott do a huge amount of analysis and they had worked out that Meggitt was probably significantly undervalued. They also thought it was under-managed, that the management was poor, had made some bad acquisitions – you name it, they were critical of it. They were very aggressive and let it be known that they were around. And they demanded to see me, so I said that I would meet one of them to discuss their views.

The guy I had agreed to meet turned up at our London office near Marble Arch with four colleagues. I kept them in the waiting room while I had a conversation with this fella. I said: "I only agreed to see you," to which he replied that he had brought his analysts along and he needed their input. So I said if I had known, I would have brought my team along as well. I asked if he was trying to intimidate me, saying, "There is only person in this world who intimidates me and that's my wife, and as far as I know she doesn't work for you." I don't think he thought that was funny.

Anyway, I had a full discussion with him and they started to poke around, and of course they then went to just about every major player in Meggitt's areas of the aerospace industry, from Honeywell and UTC in America to Safran in France, trying with the information they had to persuade one of these groups that they should buy us. But what I knew was that Meggitt had always been on these people's lists – they knew as much about the company as Elliott did. However, they always had a problem with Meggitt in that they didn't really understand the accounting and it always seemed to them that it would be slightly too expensive.

Stephen recalled that his predecessor said Meggitt was one of the top five UK takeover targets every year for his first 17 years. And my own theory is that there was also a killer factor, which was that each one of the potential bidders knew that the first person over the hill would probably not get it, because the whole thing would end up as a bun fight, a contested battle. And that would drive up the price to a level which none of the likely predators was prepared to pay. I have no hard evidence to prove it, but I think that's why, despite numerous vague overtures, Meggitt never received a firm bid over all this time.

Nonetheless, the Elliott situation galvanised me into talking to Stephen about implementing our succession plan. Luke Meynell did a full search for us, and Tony Wood emerged as an outstanding candidate. And very fortuitously, I had been introduced to Tony by Bob Cowell, a City veteran and co-founder of the investor relations consultancy Makinson Cowell. Bob was an adviser to Rolls-Royce, where Tony had run the whole of their aerospace business. Tony had left after losing out in a management reshuffle at Rolls and Bob really rated him.

Bob arranged for me to meet Tony, and I liked him. But I couldn't tell him what I was really thinking about – Stephen moving on – because it was inside information at the time. So I said that there was no opportunity at Meggitt at the moment, and we left it for three months or so. But I went back and talked to Stephen and said, 'Look, I think this is a really great guy – I've been hearing good things about him. Why don't you talk to him, have dinner with him? Without me. Have a talk and see how you get on.'

Stephen knew Tony a little bit from his Rolls-Royce days, because he was a big Meggitt customer, and they had had dinner shortly after Tony left Rolls. It was now about six months later and they met for dinner again and got on extremely well. Stephen told me that he thought Tony was absolutely right for Meggitt and said that he was ready to retire in a year or so in order to go plural. The three of us then hatched a plan: Tony would join the board as chief operating officer (COO) – it was important that he become a director because that would be a very clear signal that he was the successor. If he just joined as COO without being on the board, I don't think he would have agreed and we would have been giving no indication that there was a clear succession path. I told Tony, with Stephen's agreement, that he would become chief executive in January 2018 after a one-year handover period, during which time he would get to know the business.

In that year, with a lot of support from Stephen, Tony was able to immerse himself in the business and get to know the people, without the burdens of having to see the City and all the other stuff a chief executive has to manage. So when he took over he could absolutely hit the ground running. The good news was that the business was starting to motor as the investments began to pay off. Tony made a few operational changes, brought in a new finance director for example, and Meggitt re-entered the FTSE 100 index where it remained until Covid hit.

The way we handled the succession, Stephen, Tony and I, is seen as a text-book example of managing chief executive transition. We thought carefully about the challenge, we devised a plan to solve the problem without disrupting anything in the business, and we implemented that plan successfully. It exemplifies the way I work as a chairman. The mistake many leaders make in business is thinking that you can do it on your own. You can't. As chairman, I'm a coach and a supporter of people. My priorities are to get good people around me who can work together and who know what they're doing. And the most important person in that group is the chief executive.

Meggitt is now recognised as a really excellent business. It had some issues, including a couple of composites companies which we bought and which had teething problems. But the strategy of expanding in composites was absolutely correct because that is the way the industry is going. This part of the business will be first-rate, but it was a drag on the group for the initial period.

In January 2020, we were looking forward to a breakthrough year. Tony had really got the place buzzing and the order book was extremely healthy. I felt that this was the right time to start the process of handing over to a successor, so we announced in February that I would be stepping down as chairman before the 2021 annual meeting. No sooner had we made the announcement than Covid struck.

Every well-run company will have on its risk register the possibility of a pandemic, and Meggitt was no exception. But having the risk noted is all well and good – when Covid appeared, no-one in the industry foresaw the implications for the aviation business.

The impact of the pandemic on aviation was unprecedented, both in terms of the speed at which it struck and its scale, which was global. In April and May 2020, for the first time in the history of commercial flight, air travel came to a virtually complete standstill. In September, revenue passenger kilometres (RPKs) – which measure total airline traffic – were 72% lower than a year earlier, and they had barely risen from that trough by the year-end. ICAO, the International Civil Aviation Organisation, calculated that total lost passenger revenues for the global industry in 2020 were $371 billion.

Orders and deliveries for Airbus and Boeing collapsed with an enormous impact on their main suppliers, of which we were of course one. For the year, our revenues from civil aerospace fell by 40% and the group's operating profits halved. Similar results were reported throughout the aviation world. Even industry veterans had never seen anything like it.

Tony was very quick to respond. The first issue for any business in a crisis is cash and whether reduced profitability will trigger problems with its bank covenants. We assessed the situation thoroughly and judged that, in all but the direst circumstances, we would not need to go to our shareholders for support. Civil aerospace accounted for more than half of Meggitt's revenues and next on the action list was to downsize the business and cut costs. We reduced our headcount by about 20%, and the directors all agreed to lower their remuneration to highlight the fact that we were all in this together.

In light of the pandemic, the board asked me to stay on as chairman. I was more than happy to do so: it was the second global crisis I had faced as a chairman in 12 years, but it was very different and – for industries like civil aviation – much more damaging than the 2008 financial crash. Before the pandemic, I had come under some criticism for 'over-boarding' (holding too many chairman-ships) but the sale of Signature in early 2021 enabled me to settle that issue.

By late spring 2021, we were at last coming out of the crisis and the aviation industry was gradually recovering. The big challenge that management faced was to ramp up volumes again while recruiting the skilled workers that are essential for a highly sophisticated manufacturing operation. Tony and his team were getting to grips with this task when we received a bid approach.

In one sense, this was not a surprise – as I said, Meggitt was seen as a bid target for the whole time I had been chairman and many years before that. My fellow board members would confirm that, throughout my chairmanship, I resisted countless attempts to engage me in a conversation that might lead to a bid.

The main reason that the situation changed was Covid, which hit our share price very hard. On the eve of the pandemic, our shares were their highest-ever at almost 700p. Within three months, they had dropped to just over 200p – their lowest since the financial crisis. And while the valuations of our US competitors bounced back very quickly, that was not the case for us or other UK-listed aerospace companies.

Several of our UK peers were on the receiving end of takeover bids and in March 2021, I spoke to the *Financial Times* about the exposure of many mid-sized UK companies whose share prices were depressed by negative post-Covid sentiment in London. We knew that we were vulnerable to an approach and a number were indeed made, although we had no trouble in rejecting these.

But by mid-July 2021, our share price had only recovered to just above 400p, way below the pre-Covid level. As a board we knew that we had a fiduciary duty if a bidder came along with an exceptional price. We also knew that a sale of Meggitt would be controversial, because of the spate of other takeovers in the sector and the – in my view extremely belated – political concern about foreign ownership of important UK industrial companies.

However, a strong bidder emerged in the shape of Parker-Hannifin, the long-established, well-respected and very large American aerospace and industrial group. Of almost all the likely bidders, we had no doubt that Parker would make the best owner of Meggitt. But everything depended on the price they were prepared to offer and the conditions they were ready to accept.

There is a limit to what I can say here because at the time of writing the transaction is still live. The facts are that we negotiated a very good price – 800p a share, well above Meggitt's all-time peak. This represented a huge premium of 71% to our price immediately before the bid was announced, and of more than 90% to our price before takeover speculation started in late July. No public company board could have turned that down without flouting the interests of their owners, the shareholders.

Equally important to me was the conditionality that we placed on Parker, and which they accepted, should they be successful. They committed to increasing Meggitt's R&D investment in the UK and to maintaining its important role in the country's industrial base. This raised the benchmark for foreign bidders wishing to buy into British industry. Our conditions became even more relevant very quickly when another bidder, the ambitious US company TransDigm, made a preliminary rival offer for us at 900p a share before subsequently withdrawing.

TransDigm's intervention and the prospect of an auction prompted arbitrageurs to buy into Meggitt. This produced an interesting cameo when one US hedge fund which had taken a position insisted on speaking to me. They were very aggressive and started to tell me how I should negotiate, so I said: "On the spectrum of investors, from long-term to parasite, where would you place yourselves?" One of our brokers, who was chaperoning the meeting according to Takeover Panel rules, almost collapsed laughing. My question, which remained unanswered, brought the conversation to an abrupt end.

Despite the high price and the tough conditions, our acceptance of the Parker offer inevitably triggered criticism both of the board in general and me in particular. The latter ran along the lines of 'Nigel Rudd – the man who sold Britain', as the *Daily Mail* has commented repeatedly and very predictably. This simplistic and superficial view ignores two fundamental points – one personal, the other absolutely crucial to the future of British industry.

First, as I have made clear in this book, the circumstances surrounding the takeovers where I was chairman differed from company to company. Some transactions had similar origins – by the time I became chairman, both Pilkington and Invensys, for example, had simply lost so much competitive ground and were structurally so weak that they could not have survived and recovered as independent entities.

The only elements that all the takeovers had in common were, one, that the companies concerned were sold for very good prices which realised significantly higher value for shareholders than they could have expected in the foreseeable future, and two, that the transactions secured the future of those businesses to the benefit of their British stakeholders.

Meggitt is a completely different case from Pilkington or Invensys. It is a great business, but in world terms sub-scale. Clearly, the aerospace industry is consolidating and we would have much preferred to be a buyer than a seller in that process. But here the second point that I referred to above becomes absolutely critical.

As I wrote in relation to the Signature transaction, with a few notable exceptions industrial companies quoted in London are chronically undervalued in both absolute and relative terms. This has been the case for years – their low rating was a key element in the takeover of almost all the British motor component makers during the 1990s – and it was the main factor in driving the post-Covid acquisition of UK aerospace and other industrial companies, whether by publicly-quoted overseas buyers like Parker or by private equity firms.

Not only does this structural undervaluation leave our companies open to bids, but it seriously inhibits our ability to compete internationally in buying businesses. Moreover, as I told the *FT*, whereas US investors are prepared to see companies take on debt in order to grow both organically and by acquisition, UK-based fund managers in the post-Covid world were concerned about existing corporate debt levels, including ours.

And that is what handicapped Meggitt. As a London-quoted company, it was not feasible to make the kind of major acquisition that we needed to achieve global critical mass because any such acquisition would have been dilutive based on our relatively low share price. It remains to be seen how the bid for Meggitt evolves in the next few months, but this much is certain: while long-standing investor attitudes prevail in the UK, we will not be the last major British manufacturer that falls prey to undervaluation by the London market. The government can play a role in safeguarding investment and employment in the UK, as I pointed out in a *Sunday Times* interview, but in a free market economy they can only go so far.

19

Private Investments

I have always tried to diversify my investments both geographically and by class. Private investments are usually illiquid, so it is important to realise that cash invested in this class is for the long term.

I classify my private investments under five broad headings: Property, Start-ups, Young Companies, Medium-Sized Private Companies and Venture Capital. Over the years, I have invested in all these categories. Not all of them have come off, but overall I've done pretty well – Paolo Scaroni was kind enough to observe that if someone gave him €1 million, he would have no hesitation in asking me to invest it for him because he would know that I wasn't going to lose it and was likely to make him quite a bit of money!

My property interests are managed by my eldest son, Tim. We have office property in the north of England which I bought from receiverships during the financial crisis. I had to take a job lot, which included an empty office on the outskirts of Liverpool. We have done very well out of the package, but Liverpool was not let for some time and was therefore costing us in an empty rates charge.

Tim rang me one day to say that we had had a bid for Liverpool. What's more, it was twice the price we had paid for the site. After checking whether it was 1 April, we completed the transaction and collected the proceeds. Then, we turned our thoughts to re-investing.

I have had a love affair with South Africa for many years. Williams had business there and through that I got to know the country and its people. I have also been on the board of Sappi, the South African pulp and paper company, for many years and eventually became its chairman. It is the world's largest producer of chemical cellulose and has extensive forestry plantations producing wood fibre. It also has significant downstream interests in paper production in both Europe and North America. It's a very cyclical business, with highs and lows. But the management team and the board are of the highest standard, so it's always a pleasure to see them every three months in Johannesburg.

We have owned a home in Cape Town for many years and when the cash from the Liverpool property arrived, Tim and I decided that, instead of buying another UK property, we would look to buy a wine farm instead. Tim spent many months researching the area around Paarl and eventually we bought a neglected property but with excellent soil and topography.

With Nelson Mandela

It is said that the way to make a small fortune is to start with a large one and buy a vineyard. We have of course invested more than just the Liverpool property proceeds, but we now have one of the premier medium-sized vineyards in South Africa. The setting is stunning and we have built a Cape Dutch-style farmhouse on the site which simply takes the breath away. We don't expect to get a great return from the farm, but it is such a pleasure to own and run the estate.

I have around 20 investments in small companies since it is always wise, given the risks involved, to have a widely-spread portfolio. I have my younger son Edward as a great adviser in this area. While more than half of our investments will not really make a decent return – and some nothing at all – one or two winners make up for the all the rest. Turbo Genset, the innovative power technology company, was the biggest winner in my early forays into this asset class. At its peak, it had a market value of £750 million. I didn't get out quite at the top, but I made a very good return, nevertheless.

Brookdale Estate, the family vineyard in South Africa

Investing in these businesses is not for the faint-hearted, a fact highlighted by the saga of a start-up which is probably my best investment. It has taken the best part of 15 years before really beginning to perform.

The story started in 2004 with a call from Edward. He told me that he had been down to Swansea University and met a group of academics who were specialising in laser and Intense Pulsed Light (IPL) technology.

What they had discovered was that at certain strengths, pulsed light applied to the skin permanently removed hair follicles. They had formed a company called CyDen and wanted seed capital to see if they could commercialise their process by developing a product which could be sold to beauty salons. At the time, the only technology that could perform this function was laser-based, very cumbersome, not particularly efficient and very expensive. The CyDen business concept was that there would be both an original equipment market and a growing aftermarket, because after a series of applications or 'shots', the machine's bulb would need to be replaced.

I knew that start-ups were the riskiest investment imaginable. Very few make it through the first year, never mind becoming a viable business. However, I was intrigued by the proposition and along with a number of other high risk-takers, put together what we thought would be enough capital to take the product to market. Needless to say, things didn't work out quite like that.

We sold some machines, but not enough to be viable. The losses mounted and the inevitable request came for more money. Do you cut your losses or do you persevere? What helped my decision to continue was the government's well-designed Enterprise Investment Scheme, which was introduced by John Major's government in the mid-1990s. Under the scheme, for every £10 invested you can deduct £3 from your income for tax purposes. You can also roll over any capital gains tax (CGT) and best of all, if it all goes wrong, you can write the balance off against your income. So all in all, you are only risking 30% of your investment. Better still, if it is a success no CGT is payable and, if you were to die, no inheritance tax either.

The next turning point came about 10 years ago and five years into my investment, when we decided to change the business model completely. We had, and still have, a group of brilliant technical people and we also had designers who believed that we could produce something which could be sold for home use. The trick was to miniaturise the product while ensuring that we could actually make it at a cost that was commercially viable.

By now, we knew that we had a great product. But getting it to market on a very small budget was always going to be a challenge. I came up with a two-pronged approach, driven by my contacts at Boots and at the US consumer giant Procter & Gamble (P&G). One of these was eventually a stunning success and the other an abject failure.

First we approached Boots, which was the logical retailer for us in the UK. I knew from my chairmanship of the company that they were notoriously difficult to engage and so it proved. Meeting after meeting took place, with all sorts of ideas being discussed including the possibility that they could take a share in the business. But nothing materialised.

It soon became very apparent that for a product like ours, the margin was not there to support a viable business through High Street stores because we could not afford to give physical retailers what they wanted. We wasted months and not inconsiderable cost in working out that the only way this product could be sold profitably would be online.

Fortunately, I had met A. G. Lafley, the legendary chairman of Procter & Gamble, because he was a fellow adviser to the private equity firm Clayton, Dubilier and Rice. I contacted him and pointed out that their great rival, the Dutch group Philips, were starting to create leadership in the nascent IPL hair removal segment. I told him that Gillette and Braun, which were P&G brands, needed to be in this space and ours was the best product.

P&G got on the case and sent a team to Swansea. They appeared to be very excited about the product and its potential, and we spent time and scarce resources working with them. But as with so many large companies, there was then a management change and a new team just dropped the project.

We then had a cash crisis and realised that our existing strategy was not going to work. So we decided to change the management, and appointed Giles Davies, our chief financial officer, as chief executive. Giles brought discipline to the business and a view that we had to take our product online under our own brand, Smoothskin, to the Asia-Pacific market.

We were now starting to see growth, but as usual we needed more capital to finance it. Another funding round became inevitable – I think it was our fourth or fifth. We knew we had a business and if we were really going to take it to the next stage, we needed proper funding. The problem was that, as with all such investments, individuals simply get tired of annual fund-raising. I was prepared to go again and so were a few of the other shareholders, but we also needed fresh capital.

The Business Growth Fund was one possible source, but as I was its chairman I recognised that the conflicts there would make its involvement difficult. Then, fortunately, one of our board members introduced us to Richard Koch. Richard was the 'K' in the consultancy LEK and had been hugely successful with investments such as Betfair, the online gaming company. He is also a successful author of business books. We raised several million pounds through a highly-discounted rights issue at 15 pence a share, underwritten by Richard, myself and a few others.

We could now stop worrying about day-to-day cash problems. After a few months, the sales in China started to accelerate and cash started to flow in rather than out, followed by profit. However, we had a slight disagreement about the way forward. Some of the board thought that we should use our improving liquidity to diversify by buying other technologies adjacent to our current business. But I believed that after all this effort, we should really concentrate on maximising the potential of our core product. With Richard's support, I won the day. Since our strategy had been championed by me, I then agreed to chair the business.

On top of all this, around a year after the rights issue and completely out of the blue, P&G came back to us. They had a new team in place and they made the strategic decision to partner with us worldwide. We could retain the intellectual property and also continue to grow our own branded product.

The result has been spectacular. Over the five years to 2021, annual sales grew from £2 million to a forecast £100 million. We have moved into a new manufacturing facility in Swansea and are now one of the largest industrial employers in the City, having created 450 jobs. We are also opening a factory in China which, together with Swansea, will give us the combined capacity to produce 4 million devices a year.

The company is attracting interest from larger buyers. As I write this, shareholders have just turned down an offer of £5 a share, which values the company at more than 30 times the rights issue price. As I said – quite a saga, but with a very happy ending for all stakeholders.

20

Shooting, Golf and Other Pursuits

I'm quite competitive and have always played sport. My first game was tennis. I was a reasonable player in my early days; my mother was very keen and had played as a girl, and I played both for the school team and as a junior for Derbyshire. I enjoyed it, but when I started in business it became harder to keep up because of the way Tennis clubs are organised with midweek matches and all the rest of it.

On the golf course

So then squash became a big part of my life. It's intense and quite tactically interesting. I played for 20 or 30 years at a decent level until one day I came home on a Friday and told Lesley that I had to play four matches that weekend – because of the ladder system and the fact that you had to play the matches within a certain period of time. I played through the weekend and finished off at about 9.00 pm on the Sunday night, arrived home half-dead and Lesley said, "That's it." And my squash days were over. In any case, I was starting to get beaten by young people who were not particularly good but could outrun me, which was frustrating. It's also a bloody dangerous game if you aren't fit. I have had friends who have had strokes and that sort of thing.

In my mid-thirties, I seriously took up golf. I hadn't played much when I was young, and it is apparent to me that unless you have started early, your swing will never be that good. Michael Kirkwood describes my swing as short and punchy and claims it reflects my competitive nature. Anyway, I really enjoy the game and I have been a member of a number of clubs including Loch Lomond, which is stunning.

I was introduced to Loch Lomond by Michael, who was a member there and invited me to a Citigroup golf day, and I also played there as a guest of Barclays many times. When I first went, it was owned by an American entrepreneur who eventually went bust owing HBOS a huge amount of money, and the bank took over the club. Then the financial crisis happened and Lloyds took over HBOS. They didn't want Loch Lomond so they put it up for sale. At which point, I got a call from Barry O'Brien, who was a senior partner at the City lawyer Freshfields, saying that the members were trying to buy the business and turn it into a members' club, and they needed to raise money. And I said: "Well, what's that got to do with me?"

The clubhouse, Loch Lomond Golf Club

Barry explained that Lloyds wanted to sell the course to De Vere hotels, who would run it as a commercial operation, which would destroy the rights and enjoyment of the members. Loch Lomond had quite a lot of wealthy individuals who were prepared to support an offer and I went along to a meeting where one of the members, John Burgess who co-ran the private equity firm BC Partners, told me that they were in a bidding battle against De Vere. They felt that, because Lloyds owned a stake in De Vere, the bank would push the business in its direction.

I decided to join the members' bid and went to see Win Bischoff, who was now chairman of Lloyds and who I had of course known for many, many years going back to the early days of Williams. I told Win that we were serious, and we then managed to put the cash together – four or five of us underwrote the offer and then we syndicated it to all the members who we hoped would join us.

We got a great response: the members each put in £40,000. Lloyds then said they were prepared to accept our offer, which included a loan from the bank, on condition that I became chairman and remained there until the debt was repaid. I didn't particularly want to be chairman of a golf club, but it was the only way to clinch the deal so I agreed. That was more than 10 years ago and it has been an amazing success; it now has a surplus of about £1 million a year. We are investing in the course and in new lodges there, and you couldn't have a more beautiful place to play golf.

In Portugal with Nick Brigstocke and Bob Cowell

My other big sport is shooting. I started to shoot with Derbyshire farmers about 40 years ago and over that time I've thoroughly enjoyed the company of people I have shot with. Shooting is 70% about the people you are with and 30% the sport. I've made an enormous number of friends and had a great time over the years.

Shooting with the farmers was a hard school – instead of having big bags, there were only very small bags and unless you were very quick to shoot, you didn't get any sport at all. As a result, I developed some habits which don't perhaps conform to strict shooting etiquette. For instance, I have a reputation for being very quick to shoot birds out in front, and sometimes not only birds that are heading towards me. Michael thinks my 'leaning over' is outrageous!

In the shooting field

Nick Brigstocke once invited me to a shoot in Wales where he was drawn next to me to my left in the line, with Lord Daresbury, then chairman of De Vere Group and Aintree Racecourse, two guns further to Nick's left. The noble Lord was brought up in the gentleman's school where you only shoot birds that fly directly over your own gun or within an arc of no more than five degrees either side of you. Soon, a very high single partridge flew straight towards him, but as he raised his gun to shoot, he was astounded to see the bird fall from the sky and land dead at his feet. Unamused, he immediately looked to his right for the culprit. Being the host and a loyal adviser to Williams, Nick – who knew exactly who had fired the fatal shot – bravely shouldered the blame.

My notoriety is such that sometimes, when they draw the pegs at the start of the shoot, the other members of the party will ask, "Who's next to Nigel?" It happened the other day at Gurston Down in Wiltshire. And when I am drawn to back-gun – to stand behind the line of front guns – there is always a groan from other members of the party. I do tend to shoot some birds before they reach the front line. But it's all great fun. The only thing that is frustrating – and most people on a shoot would agree – is if you get stuck with a peg which is away from the main action. That tends to make me a bit grumpy.

However, I can also observe proprieties and remember one occasion when, again shooting with Nick, we were at a farm in Gloucestershire where we had been guests several times. At the pre-shoot briefing by the owner, he gave a firm instruction to the guns not to shoot at the one guinea fowl which was his daughter's much-loved pet.

On the second drive of the morning, a very large bird with wings the span of a jumbo jet flew out of the nearby wood. All but one of the guests recognised the guinea fowl immediately and did not raise their gun. But the executive chairman of one of the UK's leading construction companies put his gun to his shoulder and fired. His first shot missed but his second did not, and the bird hit the ground with a resounding thud. The drive ended shortly afterwards and while the embarrassed guests assembled for a pre-lunch drink, I embarked on a quick errand. Having completed it, I returned at lunchtime and presented the errant shooter of the guinea fowl with a neatly-wrapped copy of *The Pocket Guide to British Birds*.

Apart from all the outdoors stuff, I like to read. Not novels, but biographies and history in particular. My wife thinks my lack of interest in fiction means I lack imagination, but I think fact is stranger than fiction. With our home in South Africa, I have read an awful lot about the history of the country, the Zulu and Boer Wars and so on. I've also read huge amounts about the Spanish Civil War.

My interest in the Civil War dates from when I was about 17 and I embarked on my first trip abroad. Three friends, including my brother Graham, and I drove in an old Sunbeam Talbot all the way from Derby to Gibraltar. Instead of reading guide books, I thought it would be interesting to study the recent history of Spain and the Civil War in particular. The definitive history of the war was written by Hugh Thomas and I bought a copy.

George Orwell was and is my favourite author and I had read both *Animal Farm* and *Homage to Catalonia*, so I had an interest in the politics of the 1930s. General Franco was still in power then, and the era fascinates me as much today as it did 50 years ago. Today's politics have so many similarities with that period. A financial crisis which led to a distrust of democracy and the rise of populism. Unscrupulous politicians promising easy answers and resorting to ultra-nationalism are as much a feature of our world today as they were in the 1930s. Let's hope the parallels stop there.

I love reading history because, technological change notwithstanding, I think it tells you a lot about life and people and how they really behave – about human nature – and about politicians and how they get into wars almost by accident. The First World War was a classic and terrible example. You can have a trade rivalry between countries, and fighting on economic terms is all very well but then it spills over. You can see how this could happen between the US and China. As the saying goes: Those who cannot remember the past are condemned to repeat it. Which is something that company chairmen, as well as prime ministers and presidents, do well to bear in mind.

Skiing in Zermatt with Lesley

I've been a lifelong supporter of Derby County Football Club, which has had some spectacular ups and downs since I first went to a game. My father started taking me in the mid-1950s – the timing wasn't great, because Derby had just been relegated to the old Third Division North: the first time in their history that they had dropped out of the top two divisions. I remember the match was against Accrington Stanley at the old Baseball Ground, which even then was pretty decrepit as well as being a mud-heap, and which got worse until Derby finally moved to Pride Park in the late nineties.

I still go when I can – I have a season ticket for the directors' box. I've never been a director and I've never been an investor – I think that's rather a stupid thing to do with your money. But wherever I am in the world on a match day, I will be looking for their result. As I write this, Derby are heading for relegation from the Championship to League One, having been docked 21 points by the English Football League. This is the equivalent of the division where I watched my first match well over 60 years ago. Déjà vu.

Derby's great days of course were in the late sixties and the first half of the seventies after we were promoted to the old First Division under Brian Clough and Peter Taylor. They had some of the finest players of their generation – Roy McFarland, Archie Gemmill, Colin Todd, Kevin Hector, Alan Hinton and so on. They won the title twice and did well in the European Cup.

Clough and Taylor make an interesting management study. They were an outstanding combination because they complemented each other. It's always said that Taylor was very good at spotting talent and he was a controlling influence on Clough, who could be extremely eccentric. Brilliant, but eccentric.

Clough eventually fell out with the board at Derby and later moved to their arch-rival, Nottingham Forest. There's a great story, which may be apocryphal but has the ring of truth, about when Clough was at Forest and Gemmill, whom Clough had signed from Derby and who was a Scottish international, returned from the 1978 World Cup where he had scored an amazing goal against the Netherlands. It didn't do Scotland much good – they got knocked out anyway – but it was replayed endlessly on TV. He dribbled through about half the Dutch team. When he reported back for pre-season training, Clough told him to run up and down the terraces. This went on for about half an hour, at which point Gemmill is reputed to have turned to Clough and asked: "Boss – why are you making me do this?" And Clough replied: "Because you're too big-headed!"

Gemmill was an outstanding midfielder. But the other talent Clough had was to take quite ordinary players and make them exceptional. That was true at Derby and I think it was even more the case at Forest. He had an ability to make these working-class young men really believe that they could be world-class, even if they weren't. And they would walk through walls for him. He was able to get ordinary people to do extraordinary things. You get the same thing in business sometimes; there are people who are charismatic, who can lead a team and make people achieve far more in their lives than they believed possible.

Looking around the careers of some of the people I've known, I like to think that in my small way as a chairman I've done a little bit of talent-spotting – encouraging people who weren't well-known or well-established but who had the potential to become leaders, who passed through my hands and became top executives and chairmen, running major companies: Richard Baker, Paolo Scaroni, Stuart Chambers, Michael Harper, Mike Davies, Simon Pryce, Colin Matthews. The latest is Tony Wood, who I think will go on from Meggitt to even bigger things. All told, there are quite a few CEOs and chairmen with whom I've been involved during their formative years, and I've really enjoyed seeing them develop and perform at the highest level. Of the many experiences that I have enjoyed in business, that has been among the most fulfilling.

Afterword

As I write these closing lines, I am approaching my seventy-fifth birthday. My publicly-quoted chairmanships are coming to an end, 40 years after my first appointment.

I have had a wonderfully varied career, met many tremendous people and a few rogues.

I have helped to create value for shareholders and I am particularly proud of the fact that I have always left a company with a higher share price than when I started. Some spectacularly so.

I am not unhappy about stepping down from PLC boards. I find the corporate governance aspect, which increasingly dominates everything, pretty boring. When you start staring out of the boardroom window while hours are taken up with ESG reports, it really is time to go.

For her thesis at Edinburgh University, my daughter Jennifer chose the rise and fall of the conglomerate as her subject. She titled it 'A Random Walk.' I think that title could equally apply to my career.

With Lesley and the grandchildren

Select Bibliography

Entrepreneur! The ECI Ventures Guide by Tom Lloyd, Bloomsbury, 1992.

Mega-Merger Mayhem by S. J. Gray and M .C. McDermott, Paul Chapman Publishing, 1989.

The Bank That Lived a Little by Philip Augar, Allen Lane, 2018.

Venture Capital Today by Tony Lorenz, Woodhead Faulkner, 1985.

Sir Nigel Rudd interviews in the *Daily Telegraph*, *Management Today*, *Sunday Business*, and *Sunday Times* 1994–2010.

Index